Praying through the Window III

The Unreached Peoples

Edited by
Patrick Johnstone, John Hanna, & Marti Smith

Helping a New Generation Enter a New Land
10 West Dry Creek Circle • Littleton, CO 80120

PUBLISHING
A Ministry Of Youth With A Mission
P.O. Box 55787, Seattle, WA 98155

Publishing Information

Praying Through the Window III: The Unreached Peoples

ISBN 0-927545-98-5

Published by YWAM Publishing, a ministry of Youth With A Mission, PO Box 55787, Seattle WA 98155, USA. For a free catalogue of books and materials, write the above address or call: 1-206-771-1153 or 1-800-922-2143.

Written and Edited by Caleb Project, John Hanna, Managing Editor, 10 W. Dry Creek Circle, Littleton CO 80120, USA. For a free resource list, write the above address or e-mail to info@cproject.com.

Photos throughout this book courtesy and © Mike Staub and Caleb Project unless otherwise noted.

Cover photos courtesy Caleb Project and OMF International.

Bible verses taken from the HOLY BIBLE: NEW INTERNATIONAL VERSION © 1978 by the New York International Bible Society, used by permission of Zondervan Bible Publishers, Grand Rapids, Michigan, USA.

Printed in the United States of America.

Dedication

*This book is dedicated to those who are pouring out their lives,
ministering to the unreached peoples of
the 10/40 Window, despite great opposition
and difficult circumstances.*

*Without their sacrifice and service,
our prayers would be hollow words,
but together with their labour
we can all look with hope,
anticipating the day of Christ's return.*

Foreword

by Dr. C. Peter Wagner

Co-ordinator, AD2000 United Prayer Track

The book in your hands has the potential to become a powerful force moving the body of Christ toward completing Jesus' Great Commission. This prayer guide brings to life the goal of "a church for every people and the gospel for every person by AD 2000."

The United Prayer Track of the AD2000 and Beyond Movement operates on the premise that *at its core, world evangelisation is an engagement of the enemy in spiritual warfare.* Jesus' commission to the Apostle Paul on the Damascus Road was to go to the world's *ethne,* or in modern translation, to the "unreached peoples," and to "turn them from the power of Satan to God." Such an assignment depends on spiritual warfare.

The premise also has a corollary: *the central, most powerful, weapon of spiritual warfare is prayer.* The role of the United Prayer Track can be stated very simply. We must do whatever it takes to motivate and mobilise God's people everywhere for massive, prevailing, powerful, and effective prayer for the lost. Without this, there is little chance of even approaching the completion of the Great Commission in our lifetime.

But it is happening right before our eyes! God is raising up praying people across geographic, denominational, racial, and generational lines. Prayer movements and prayer ministries are springing up on every continent. The numbers of praying people are swelling. The prayer movement is out of control!

To serve the prayer movement and to provide whatever co-ordination is possible, the United Prayer Track regularly schedules high-profile prayer campaigns. Some are one-time events, and some are repeated every year. New ones are constantly added. Every year we promote the *March for Jesus* in which huge numbers of believers take to the streets with public prayers of praise and declaration of the lordship of Jesus Christ. Some marches include more than one million participants. Also each year during the 30 days of the Muslim fast of Ramadan, millions of Christians pray together for the salvation of Muslims.

We call 1996 the year to "heal the land." Even as I write, numerous acts of corporate repentance and reconciliation are being carried out in many parts of the world. White Americans are repenting for cruel massacres of American Indians and for more than 350 broken treaties. Japanese are repenting for the bombing of Pearl Harbour. Brazilians are repenting for robbing territory in Paraguay. The largest corporate reconciliation is the Reconciliation Walk, a four-year project which began Easter 1996 in Cologne, Germany, to conclude in Jerusalem in July, 1999. Thousands of believers are walking the routes of the First Crusade, repenting for the sins of Christians against Muslims and Jews.

This book will orient you to the largest of all the prayer projects that the United Prayer Track has yet undertaken, *Praying through the Window III*.

Praying through the Window III builds on the world-wide prayer initiative focused on the 62 countries of the 10/40 Window in October 1993 and the global prayer concentrated on the 100 "Gateway Cities" of the 10/40 Window in October 1995. Now many of the unreached peoples of the 10/40 Window are spotlighted for prayer. Some 20 million people participated in the first effort, and 30 million in the second. This is extremely encouraging.

Is it possible that 50 million Christians might join this third effort, calling out to the Creator for the establishment of his kingdom among the unreached peoples? What better chance could we possibly have to see millions of lost people being turned from the power of Satan to God? United prayer for the lost is the tool of the ages and the tool for today!

Acknowledgements

It is a miracle that this book exists at all. The Lord interrupted my life and divinely prepared Caleb Project. Then, Jesus intervened at each step to keep the project going as we hit walls trying to find information, photos, writers, editors, and other resources. However, after prayer, we found these walls disappeared.

Also, this book could not have come about except for the scores of people before us, researching the plight of the unreached peoples. Because of the U.S. Center for World Mission, the *Perspectives on the World Christian Movement* course, and so many others, it is becoming well-known. What is more, people-group concepts have moved out of theory and into practice, seen most tangibly in the AD2000 movement meetings like GCOWE (the Global Consultation on World Evangelization) and the previous *Praying through the Window* projects in 1993 and 1995. This project depended on their prayers and the momentum gained from these projects. Thanks to Stephen Hagman, Mark Wilson, and Beverly Pegues for bringing together the *100 Gateway Cities* prayer focus in 1995, and Stephen Hagman's groundbreaking work in 1993 on the *62 Countries of the 10/40 Window* prayer guide. Due to you and the thousands who helped with promotion, there is a growing and fruitful movement of prayer spanning the globe. Also of significant mention here are the ongoing labours of the *Global Prayer Digest*, most recently headed by Keith Carey. For years now, they have stimulated committed, fervent prayer for the unreached peoples. More than 13 years ago God used you to open my eyes in prayer for unreached peoples. Thanks!

Many others also contributed to the background information for this book, including Robert Nance who thoughtfully compiled a variety of obvious sources into files now bearing his name on the Internet. Others, like the fearless corps of Southern Baptist missionary-researchers, have compiled and co-ordinated their work, making it available to us all. Also, the linguistic researchers attached to SIL, Wycliffe, and others have made great strides cataloguing the languages of the world. My gratitude goes to them and Ronald Rowland (PIN), YWAM, HCJB, FEBC, OMF, CMA, the *Jesus* film Project, IBS, and so many others. Their work has become the foundation for a new generation of researchers answering the call of Luis Bush for Joshua Project 2000. They will build on this book and the databases, providing invaluable information to church planters, relief workers, and prayer warriors in the next few years.

Much of the organisation of this book came directly from the work of Patrick Johnstone. One of Patrick's life goals has been to describe the peoples of the world and his work on affinity blocs and people-group clusters is the basis for this guide. Patrick, may your dreams of churches for every bloc, cluster, people, and sub-group come true!

Acknowledging the foundation of this book could not be complete without mentioning the vision of the *Praying through the Window* committee which has given leadership to this campaign these six years. Moreover, they have provided vital resources, including money and personnel, to see it succeed. Thanks go to the Christian Broadcasting Network (CBN), Michael Little specifically, Peter and Doris Wagner, Luis Bush, and John Robb among others.

Also of significant note are Bob and Kathryn Carlton. Not only have they produced the exemplary *Praying through the Window* videos, but Bob has been my vital link to the outside world. Through his work (together with associates at YWAM Publishing, especially Michelle Drake), arrangements have been made for this book to be translated into 22 languages and be distributed world-wide. Thanks, Bob, for managing the deck topside so I could find something to print.

The greatest challenge preparing to write was finding information beyond the statistics. There are many who helped us put hearts to the numbers, including Gabriella & the Bethany World Prayer Center, Jack & Cathy Ollis, Bep & our YWAM friends, OBJ at the Nirobi Interfaith Research Centre, AMO's Paul Hattaway, and Doug Lucas and the Brigada folks. Thanks! Also of great assistance were Yana Ahn, Scott S., Russ Irwin, Roy T., Richard LaFountain, friends of the Komering, Oswald Buchannan, Nanci H., Mike Kroupa, Michael Densmoor, Melody F., Matt B., Mark H., John Kless, John N., Irving Sylvia, Don Davis, Charles F., Bruce Sidebotham, Brent Fulton, Battle Brown, and Alexander Mares-Manton. These men and women got us the information we needed to be able to write.

Amazingly, at the beginning of the week when we gave writing assignments all we had was an outline and stacks of files. At the end of the following week we had a book. Thanks, team: Shane Bennett, Patty Fraats, our friends of the Amdo, Nancy Floyd, Mrs. W, Mike & Leah Fen, Marti Smith, Keith Carey, Gwen Hanna, Greg Purnell, Gregory Fritz, Debbie Lee, Deb Sanders, Dave Moody, Dave Hemperly, Chris Istrati, and Amy Barstad. Blessings upon your households! Then, what was written needed to be checked, corrected, expanded, checked again for security, style, grammar, spelling, and punctuation. Much of this was accomplished by people already mentioned, but there are many others, too. However, of special note were Viju Abraham, Paul Hattaway, OBJ, Bep, RUN Ministries, Friends of Turkey, CBI, and TEAM. If a picture is worth a thousand words, then the following people have added more to this book than any others. Thanks, Mr. Staub, Kim Williamson, Ron Geerling (CRWM), and Bob Fetherlin (C&MA).

Most critical of all these, Marti Smith co-ordinated all the assembly and editing of these profiles. Without her tireless effort, you indeed would have no book in front of you at all. Thank you, Marti, for pouring yourself out in this way, helping bring life to these (at times) rather flat words. May the God of all grace meet you in all your needs, filling you to the fullness in him!

Thanks also goes to my patient wife and daughter who selflessly gave me freedom to finish this book.

It would be impossible to thank everyone who helped make this project possible, and I fear that some were even inadvertently overlooked. Thank you also!

Thank you for taking the time to pray for these peoples and giving of your heart to join in prayer for those who are yet to know God's saving grace...

With Gratitude,

John Hanna, Managing Editor.

Table of Contents

People Groups With No Known Christians or Missionaries Working With Them.

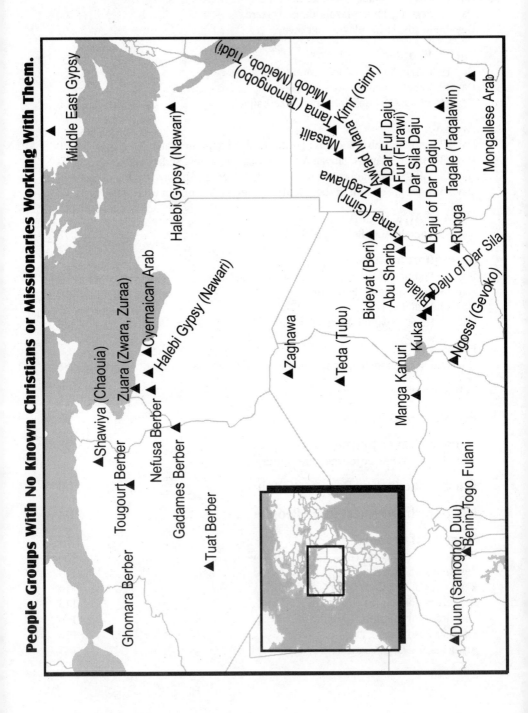

Middle East Gypsy

Halebi Gypsy (Nawari)

Cyernaican Arab

Halebi Gypsy (Nawari)

Shawiya (Chaouia)

Zuara (Zwara, Zuraa)

Tougourt Berber

Nefusa Berber

Gadames Berber

Ghomara Berber

Tuat Berber

Zaghawa

Teda (Tubu)

Manga Kanuri

Duun (Samogho, Duu)

Benin-Togo Fulani

Bideyat (Beri)

Abu Sharib

Kuka

Bilala

Daju of Dar Sila

Ngossi (Gevoko)

Kimr (Gimr)

Tama (Tamongobo)
Midob (Meidob, Tiddi)

Masalit

Awied Mana

Zaghawa

Tama (Gimr)

Dar Fur Daju

Fur (Furawi)

Dar Sila Daju

Daju of Dar Dadju

Runga

Tagale (Taqalawin)

Daju of Dar Dadju

Mongallese Arab

- 10 -

Part I

The History of Praying through the Window

by Ted Haggard
Senior Pastor, New Life Church

The majority of the people in the world who have not had the chance to hear the gospel even once live in a belt that stretches across North Africa, the Middle East, India, and Asia. Missions researchers call this area the *10/40 Window*. Today they are asking the following questions:

What is in the 10/40 Window that makes it difficult to reach people for Christ?
What are the most effective means of reaching these people?
Who is most effective in reaching the people of the 10/40 Window?

Answers to these questions are difficult. Research shows that while 97 percent of the people who live in the least-evangelised countries are located in the 10/40 Window, about one percent of missions funding is spent there. Why is this so? Churches and mission agencies answer, "We can't effectively work there." The spiritual, political, and economic realities of the 10/40 Window seem overwhelming. We need a spiritual breakthrough.

In 1992, Dr. C. Peter Wagner, co-ordinator of the AD2000 United Prayer Track, called for a million intercessors to pray for effective evangelism in the 62 countries of the 10/40 Window. This effort, *Praying through the Window I*, moved more than 20 million intercessors from 105 nations, to pray for the 10/40 Window countries during the month of October 1993. Teams from 32 nations actually visited the 10/40 Window countries to pray on-site in what have been called *prayer journeys*.

The spiritual response within the Window was immediate. Countries from Albania to Indonesia reported signs of greater freedom for the gospel. Key national leaders experienced dreams and visions of Christ. Demonic powers were weakened. Details of this prayer effort are documented in the Christian Information Network's *WindoWatchman* (see appendix). Although greatly encouraged by the growth of God's kingdom in the 10/40 Window, intercessors were sobered by the continuing needs. This prompted a second global prayer effort, *Praying through the Window II*, calling millions to pray for 100 "Gateway Cities" in the 10/40 Window in October, 1995.

The overwhelming response of intercessors world-wide in 1993 led the Prayer Committee to encourage greater participation in the 1995 prayer initiative. This resulted in 2,465 known prayer journeyers travelling to Gateway Cities from 48 countries, as 36.7 million intercessors prayed for massive evangelism in the 10/40 Window.

According to mission strategist Fred Markert, director of Youth With A Mission's Strategic Frontiers division, the church population of Gambia, Guinea Bissau, and

Mali is growing twice as fast as the overall population! The church in China now tops 100 million, 25 million of whom are new converts from the last four years. The Chinese Communist Party wrote a letter reminding all its members that they are Atheists because too many were converting to Christianity!

Churches in the 10/40 Window may owe some of their growth to the increase in miracles and unusual manifestations since the 1993 prayer effort. When the sole believer in a Muslim village in North India died, he was buried in a cemetery on top of a hill outside the village. After returning home, his neighbours saw a stranger walk away from the cemetery, come into the village and look into many of the houses. That day a *Jesus* film team came to the area. Politely watching the film, the villagers were amazed by the scene of Christ's baptism. Seeing the face of Jesus, they exclaimed, "That's the man we saw going from house to house!" They all got saved! In India, 15,000 new believers are baptised each day. Although India's huge needs continue, six percent of the population is now Christian!

The year of October 1, 1996, to October 31, 1997, has been designated by the AD2000 United Prayer Track as *Praying through the Window III*. This global effort focuses on the 10/40 Window's thousands of unreached people groups—ethno-linguistic groups with no indigenous gospel witness. Unreached men and women may live an entire lifetime without ever hearing that Jesus Christ came to earth to rescue them.

Use this book as a guide to pray for these groups. As the Spirit of the Lord directs, many of you will be called to go to the 10/40 Window to help fulfill the Great Commission there. As millions join you in prayer, more and more people living in the 10/40 Window will have a chance to hear the life-giving gospel.

Joshua Project 2000

by Luis Bush
International Director, AD2000 and Beyond Movement

The *10/40 Window* is home to the majority of the world's Muslims, Hindus, and Buddhists. It is the undeniable task of the church to join God the Father in bringing the gospel to these peoples.

With hearts of faith, many of God's servants world-wide believe that we are the "Joshua generation," called to spiritually "inherit the lands" of the remaining unreached peoples through church planting. This is the time. The end of the story has already been told. "...I looked and there before me was a great multitude that no one could count, from every nation, tribe, people and language, standing before the throne and in front of the Lamb..." (Revelation 7:9).

The *Praying through the Window III* project lays the foundation for a global strategic initiative called *Joshua Project 2000*. Joshua Project 2000 is an international co-operative strategy focused on the least-evangelised peoples of the world. We are hoping that every church, agency, denomination, and Christians from every country in the world will work toward the goal of "A church for every people and the gospel for every person by AD2000." We are trusting God for reproducing churches of at least 100 believers in each of the Joshua Project 2000 peoples by December 31, 2000. Your prayers are the foundation in this effort.

The people groups profiled in this book are based on a list compiled by Joshua Project 2000 and included in the appendix of this book. The Joshua Project 2000 list of peoples attempts to identify those people groups most in need of a church-planting movement. The list includes more than 2000 people groups, each with a population of at least 10,000, with less than five percent Christians. Most are distinguished by ethnicity and language.

Prayer was instrumental in developing this list. On November 21, 1994, researchers from around the world gathered in an extraordinary meeting. They represented a wide range of perspectives. The researchers devoted the first half of their meeting to prayer. One by one, each participant read a verse from John 17 and prayed that verse to the Lord.

In a spirit of unity researchers drafted the document that serves as the foundation for the Joshua Project 2000 peoples' list today. The document stated: "Whereas we agree that Jesus commands us to share the gospel with the whole world, and to ensure that every people group or 'nation' (Matthew 28:20) in the whole world is discipled.... We therefore, representing various research initiatives...do now resolve in wholehearted agreement without any reservation, to invite the Christian community world-wide to the following:

1. To challenge their constituencies towards achieving the goal of a church for every people and the gospel for every person by the year 2000 (i.e., by December 31, 2000).

2. To use ethno-linguistic peoples within a country…as our current frame of reference for assessing the task and for mobilising the world-wide church for prayer and mission involvement.

3. To fulfil Christ's mandate to make disciples of the nations (ethne) and the AD2000 goal of a church for every people by the year 2000,…[we will] publish a list of all the peoples that are deemed to be most needing a church-planting movement in their midst."

For strategic purposes, the closely related peoples on the list can be clustered together. The 129 people-group names in this book serve as names for clusters of people groups, and thus represent the majority of the Joshua Project 2000 peoples.

Praying for these peoples and committing to take the gospel to them allows us to be a channel of blessing to the world. The Scriptures tell us of a man named Obed-Edom. "The ark of God remained with the family of Obed-Edom in his house for three months, and the LORD blessed his household and everything he had" (1 Chronicles 13:14). After the ark was taken to Jerusalem, Obed-Edom also moved. He became a gatekeeper to the house of the Lord (1 Chronicles 26:15).

Like Obed-Edom, we have experienced the blessings of the Lord. Let us choose, like him, to open the gates of this blessing to others, as we pray for the world's unreached people groups. Let us pray that the blessings of God may flow into each of these peoples so that each person may have a valid opportunity to experience the truth and saving power of Jesus Christ.

The Challenge of the Unreached Peoples

by John Robb
Unreached Peoples Program Director, World Vision International

Leaning over a steaming cup of black Russian coffee in a Moscow hotel, I ask my bushy-haired, olive-skinned acquaintance whether he had ever heard of Jesus. "Oh, yes," he replies, instantly, "Wasn't he a Japanese?"

I was appalled that an educated man like Dr. M. could have so little knowledge of the greatest person in human history. But Dr. M. was a Muslim from the Caucasus, an area of the 10/40 Window where a multitude of unreached people groups live. Though surprising, it was understandable that he had not yet been exposed to the love and truth of Jesus. His people group had been cut off from this knowledge for centuries by religious, cultural, and political walls. There may be Christians living in his city, but there are few, if any, of his own people who are Christian.

This story has a happy ending! Later, after reading the New Testament, he not only came to a deep faith himself but led his brother, father, and grandfather to Christ as well, and wrote a tract describing biblical stories of healing and circulated it to his patients and friends back home. Still, most in the 10/40 Window have no opportunity to hear of the Person of persons.

What exactly *is* a people group? Often the members of a people group have their own language or dialect, and a different ethnicity from people around them. Sometimes we use the term "ethno-linguistic" peoples to reflect these differences. Sometimes, as in many parts of India, class or occupation barriers are more significant than language or ethnicity. From the standpoint of evangelism, a people group is "the largest group within which the gospel can flow along natural lines without encountering barriers of understanding or acceptance." This simply means that unless the gospel comes from someone within one's own people group, it is foreign. For members of an unreached people group to receive the gospel, it must be communicated across these cultural divides.

Dr. M's lack of knowledge of Christ is typical for unreached peoples and in much of the 10/40 Window. There are many reasons for this. One is the hostility of religious and political authorities who feel threatened, afraid that Christianity will diminish their power. In places like Iran and Sudan, authorities have tried to eradicate the Christian movement.

Spiritual oppression is another cause. The apostle Paul said "the god of this world has blinded the minds of the unbelievers so they will not believe in the gospel" (2 Corinthians 4:4). Jesus tells us that the spiritual "strongman" must be bound before his house can be plundered (Mark 3:27). The false gods, principalities, and powers working through false religious systems give non-believers the wrong idea about Christians. They blind whole peoples and keep them in the dark about Jesus.

Many of the 800 million people who are illiterate live in the 10/40 Window, unable to read the New Testament or any Christian literature. More than 80 percent of the world's poorest people live in the Window; for them daily life is a struggle for survival. Many are malnourished, have no access to health care of any kind, nor safe, clean water to drink. In the Window, often the lost are the poor and the poor are the lost. Of such people Mahatma Gandhi said, "There are some people so poor that God can only appear to them in the form of bread."

Among the unreached peoples the greatest reason for misunderstanding or not knowing of Jesus Christ is the absence of active Christians who speak their languages and can share the truth about Jesus in a culturally appropriate manner. For example, a Turkmen might find an example of a Russian church, but he or she has no example of a culturally Turkmen church. Indeed this is the very definition of an unreached people: they are without an indigenous Christian movement in large enough numbers and with adequate resources to evangelise the rest of their group. Yet given the chance to hear, many will respond as Dr. M. did. They simply have not had a suitable opportunity to hear. A missionary friend of mine rode Pakistan's buses and trains every day for many years in order to share Jesus Christ with his fellow passengers. Only once in all those years did one of them acknowledge having heard the gospel before.

Five years ago, two churches in my home town "adopted" an unreached people in Central Asia. At that time there were only two known Christians in the people group, and no known mission efforts to reach the group. Some travelled to Central Asia through a sister-city program in order to build relationships. Cultural research assisted informed, focused prayer. As the churches prayed, they got involved in other ways: providing medical equipment and participating in youth and musicians exchanges. God brought together a partnership now involving more than 20 agencies and churches. The New Testament has been translated and the indigenous church has now grown substantially, all in less than five years!

Accept the challenge from the Lord of the church to get involved personally with other believers in a network of churches and agencies. Choose a people group not likely to be chosen by others, find out all you can learn about them, and share it with your church. As you pray for them, God will lead you to creative ways to make a difference. Consider sending a research or prayer team to visit and build relationships, raising financial support for local Christian workers, or meeting a tangible need like medical supplies. The sky is the limit! As you pray, ask God to give you his perspective and his heart for this people. God's heart breaks over the lostness and suffering of whole peoples without the knowledge of his son. Tens of millions like Dr. M. from among the remaining unreached peoples are still waiting for someone to come to them.

Building Prayer into Your Local Church

By Larry Stockstill

Pastor of the Bethany World Prayer Center, Baton Rouge, Louisiana

Bethany World Prayer Center has taken on the task of mobilising their congregation to make frontier missions a top priority. The church's 300 cell groups are committed to praying for the unreached peoples every week. To assist prayer and missions efforts, the Bethany World Prayer Center has taken up the challenge of producing profiles on roughly 1700 of the unreached peoples of the world.

Do you remember Nehemiah? Under his leadership the people of Israel built a wall. Those of us who are pastors face a task similar to his, but the wall we build is made of prayer instead of bricks and mortar. As we build prayer into our local churches, we can follow the process Nehemiah used to build Jerusalem's defences.

Nehemiah's momentum came from **vision**. He saw the problem. When he heard about Jerusalem's condition, he sat down and wept, and fasted and prayed before the God of heaven (Nehemiah 1:4). As I see the needs of the world, my heart is broken. Fully persuaded of the massive, global disaster toward which the three billion unreached are eternally moving, I'm motivated to tell others. The 3.5 billion unreached people on earth would form a single file line that would stretch around the equator 25 times! Can you picture 25 lines of Christless people, trampling endlessly toward hell? Let that vision stay with you day and night.

But Nehemiah also had hope, and he moved others to action. His vision led to **communication**. Gathering the leaders together, Nehemiah said, "Come, let us build up the world for Jerusalem" (Nehemiah 2:17). Pastors today have the opportunity to plant in the soul of every member a vision for the unreached. May our preaching communicate effectively! May our churches see with us the immensity of the need, then respond, "Let us rise up and build" (Nehemiah 2:18).

The book you are holding can enable each Christian to begin visualising the unseen masses of unreached people, which were before only names on a list. Use pictures, maps, profiles, videos, live missionaries, or your own short-term ministry teams to keep the vision of the unreached before the eyes of the local church. At the Bethany World Prayer Center, we often add dramas to our Sunday morning services. Our actors represent members of an unreached people group, dressed in full native dress and talking to themselves out loud about how frustrated and desperate they are for reality and the knowledge of the living God. As the pastor, look for creative ways to keep the vision of the unreached ever before your flock.

Nehemiah followed his challenge with **delegation**. He gave ordinary people a part in the massive job. Our churches are full of people who have no purpose, who tramp in and out of services week after week with a focus on themselves. Help them find their part. Instead of trying to build the entire thing, Nehemiah gave each family one section of the wall. If you would mobilise your church to pray for the unreached, try giving one people group to each cell group, Bible class, men's meeting or ladies' prayer group. Spread the job across your entire congregation, not just to a few that gather faithfully as the "missions committee." Let each group do their own research and study in the local library to enhance their vision and present it to the church. We are seldom dedicated to pray for anything for which we do not feel a sense of ownership.

Nehemiah's people had "a mind to work" and saw the significance of their task. They knew they might face opposition, and built with one hand and held a sword with the other. They slept in their clothes for 52 days. A sense of urgency and warfare kept their effort alive. Praying for the unreached is a means of *warfare* against the forces of darkness. Our congregations need to know that releasing these nations from the enshrouding darkness that has held them for thousands of years will take a spiritual battle. Help them see that their prayers are opposed by the rulers of the darkness of this world. Godless ideas, false gods, and demonic worship must be confronted in the spirit realm before missionary activity will ever be effective and before Christ's return.

The result of Nehemiah's vision, communication, delegation, and warfare was a mighty, sustained effort that persevered to the end. As you and your church set aside this time to pray for the final frontiers of missions, gear up for battle. Prayer will be the key that unlocks the doors shut tightly for centuries. Inside those doors are billions of lost souls, and your prayer will be a key to their eternal life!

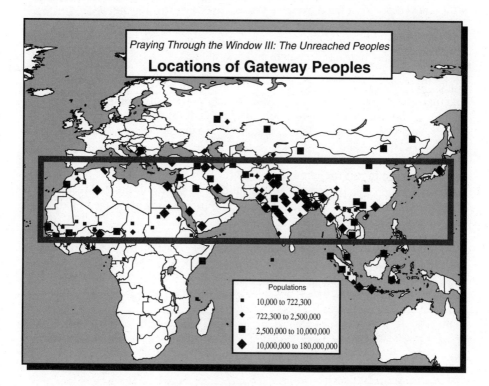

Praying Through the Window III: The Unreached Peoples
Locations of Gateway Peoples

Populations

- ▪ 10,000 to 722,300
- ◆ 722,300 to 2,500,000
- ■ 2,500,000 to 10,000,000
- ◆ 10,000,000 to 180,000,000

Jesus' Model of Prayer

by Dr. Sang-Bok Kim

Executive Director, Torch Missions Centre;
Senior Pastor, Hallelujah Christian Church, Seoul, Korea

Jesus began his public life with prayer. During his baptism, at the moment of prayer, heaven was opened, the Holy Spirit descended on him, and the voice of God was heard from heaven. It is the same for us: as soon as we begin to pray, that is the moment heaven is opened. God and man come into perfect communion. Human limitations disappear, and the God of the universe steps in. If we realised what prayer does for us, we would more frequently come into his presence through prayers, wouldn't we?

Not only do the heavens open when we pray, but the Holy Spirit descends upon us. How exciting to know this truth! Jesus could only be in one place at one time, but the comforter he sent, the Holy Spirit, can be with us any place and any time. The Holy Spirit will empower us as we pray. When Jesus prayed, he heard the sweet voice of his Father God, saying, "This is my beloved Son." How we all wish to hear God's assuring words of love! All these things happen when we pray. Great orators may move the multitude of people, but even the simplest prayer speaks straight to the heart of God.

Jesus enjoyed prayer alone in solitary places. He often went to a mountain to pray, and continued all night in prayer to God. Before important decisions such as choosing his apostles, he talked to his Father. Even when he was with his disciples, he would separate himself from them and pray alone.

Sometimes he prayed with a small group of his disciples. We can also come together with two or three of our friends for prayer. Jesus promised that when two or three gather together and pray, God hears them. Jesus not only prayed with his friends, he prayed for them. He told Simon, "I have prayed for you that your faith may not fail" (Luke 22:32).

Paul also prayed for his friends, and wanted them to know that he was praying for them. Again and again he prayed for the churches begun by his mission team and encouraged them with his prayers. Likewise, our friends are encouraged to know that we are interceding for them.

Jesus did not pray to get what he wanted, but to receive strength to fulfil the will of the Father. He was in perfect harmony with his Father. When he faced the cross he was able to say, "Father, if you are willing, take this cup from me; yet not my will, but yours be done" (Luke 22:42). Prayer helps us do the will of God.

In his prayers, Jesus was also able to forgive those who crucified him. Jesus said, "Father, forgive them, for they do not know what they are doing" (Luke 23:34a). How can we forgive those who hurt us? Only prayer can do it.

Jesus' last act was a prayer, the natural ending to a life of prayer. We, too, can commit ourselves to God as he did. To Jesus, prayer was as natural as breathing. If we earnestly desire to be more like Jesus, let us follow his pattern.

Prayer has no financial cost. It requires no academic degrees. Prayer does not demand a cathedral, bent knees, or even closed eyes. Wherever and whenever one humbly slips into the presence of the Lord, he is in touch with our wonderful God. Jesus began his ministry with prayer, he continued to pray, and ended his life with prayer. If Jesus lived in prayer, how much more do we need to pray?

We may help our neighbours with our money and our strength, but having done so, we will run out of money and strength. Prayer is different. By prayer we can unleash God's limitless resources. Even if we are limited, prayer is limitless because God is limitless.

Affinity Blocs and the Unreached Peoples

by Patrick Johnstone
Author, *Operation World*

What do these terms mean? Instead of confusing you, these terms should help you come to grips with the many names of peoples that still need to be evangelised. You may not have heard of many of the names listed in the appendix of this book!

Over these last two decades researchers have, for the first time, painstakingly listed the indigenous and immigrant peoples in every country of the world. Diagram 1 shows the 12,000 peoples in the world. These peoples are divided into four categories according to their state of evangelisation. The numbers are rounded to the nearest 1000 for ease of understanding. You will see that we are far further ahead in reaching all the peoples of the world than many had realised. About half the peoples of the world are already, at least nominally, Christian. Another quarter have large Christian minorities, and Christianity is somewhat accepted by the culture. The other quarter represent peoples where the church is still small, insignificant, or even non-existent and where pioneer evangelism and church planting is still needed. The Joshua Project list includes peoples with a population greater than 10,000 and less than two percent evangelical. There are 1,746 peoples in this list. These peoples comprise the heavily shaded portions of the bars. There are many other peoples of less than 10,000 population that are not included in the Joshua Project list, but many of these are actually off-shoots of listed peoples separated by political boundaries.

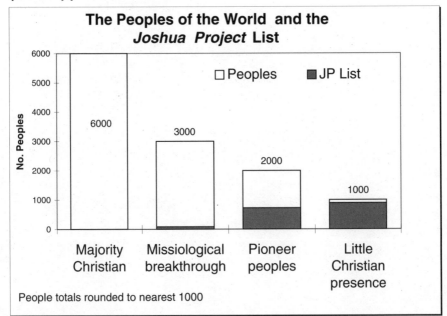

The Peoples of the World and the *Joshua Project* List

People totals rounded to nearest 1000

It helps us to put these names into groups with similarities. Almost all the Joshua Project peoples either live in or near the 10/40 Window or have migrated from these areas to countries around the world. There are 11 major blocs of peoples in the Window. We call these *Affinity Blocs*. The remaining unreached peoples, spread out around the world, comprise a twelfth Bloc. Each of these Blocs share similarities in language, culture, religion, politics, geography, and history. Diagram 2 shows these 12 Affinity Blocs. Each Bloc has two bars; one to show the number of Joshua Project people groups and the other to show their population. It is interesting to see that the Indian sub-continent contains nearly half of the world's least-evangelised individuals.

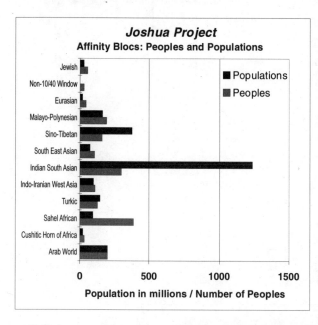

Within each Affinity Bloc we can make smaller groupings of peoples which are more closely related and which often have a common name. We have defined these groupings as *Gateway People Clusters* or GPCs; *Gateway* because they represent a gateway for the gospel by prayer and evangelisation; and *Clusters* because each represents many subgroups. The 140 GPCs include more than 75 percent of all the Joshua Project peoples. Of these, 129 have been included in this book for prayer. You will find many names that you may recognise, such as the Turks, Tibetans, Mongolians, or Persians, but even these clusters include separate people groups you may have never heard of—peoples distinguished by such factors as language, country of residence, or religion. The appendix at the end of this book includes a complete list of all the people groups which make up each GPC. Each one needs prayer, and also a variety of missions effort, including witnesses who will go to them make disciples for Jesus.

As you pray through each day, you will be impacting the many peoples of the world that are not yet adequately evangelised. This book gives only a small amount of prayer information. Profiles of greater depth are also available to assist in your prayers.

We have an immense, but finishable task, and I believe through prayer and obedience to the Great Commission we can see church-planting initiatives launched for every one of the peoples in this book by the end of the year 2000.

People Groups with No Known Christians or Missionaries Working with Them.

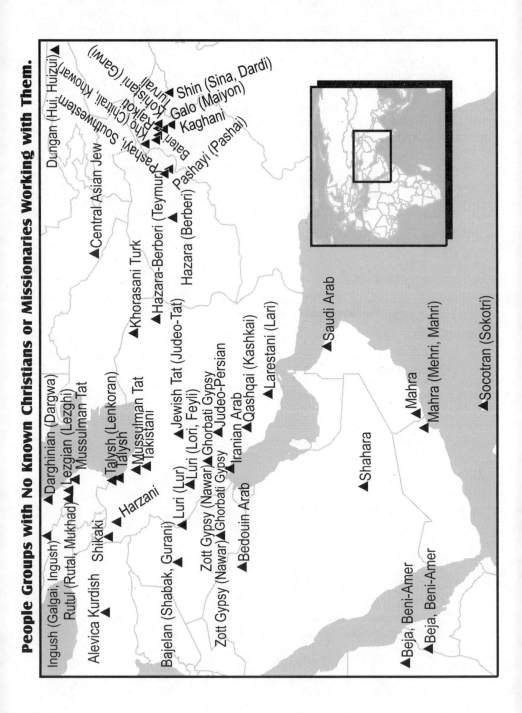

Dungan (Hui, Huizui)

Kho (Chitrali, Khowar, Southwestern,
Kohistani (Garwi)
Kohistani (Garwi)
Rajkoti
Baten
Pashayi,
Shin (Sina, Dardi)
Galo (Maiyon)
Kaghani
Pashayi (Pashai)
Pashayi (Pashai)

Central Asian Jew

Hazara-Berberi (Teymur)
Pashayi
Hazara (Berberi)

Khorasani Turk

Jewish Tat (Judeo-Tat)

Larestani (Lari)

Saudi Arab

Darghinian (Dargwa)
Ingush (Galgai, Ingush)
Lezgian (Lezghi)
Rutul (Rutal, Mukhad)
Mussulman Tat

Talysh (Lenkoran)
Talysh
Mussulman Tat
Takistani

Alevica Kurdish   Shikaki

Harzani

Qashqai (Kashkai)

Ghorbati Gypsy
Judeo-Persian

Mahra

Mahra (Mehri, Mahri)

Bajelan (Shabak, Gurani)

Luri (Lur)
Luri (Lori, Feyli)
Zott Gypsy (Nawar)
Ghorbati Gypsy
Iranian Arab

Shahara

Socotran (Sokotri)

Zott Gypsy (Nawar)
Bedouin Arab

Beja, Beni-Amer

Beja, Beni-Amer

Part II

Strategies to Pray

This prayer guide is an invitation for you to join with millions of your brothers and sisters in the body of Christ from around the world and to pray for ethnic groups which are today largely beyond the reach of the gospel. If individuals commit to pray for these groups, this project will be a success. However, if we can call one another together to meet in small groups and large, how much more will our prayers reap a harvest in the heavenlies?

Whether you use this prayer guide in your personal prayer time, family devotions, a prayer group at church, school, or work, or with some larger group, adding creativity can make your prayer time memorable and enjoyable. Prayer groups can be built with people from all kinds of backgrounds, ages, and experience. Grandmothers, kids, couples, singles, new believers, and mature Christians all have a contribution to make.

Go Visual

Often using visual aids helps encourage prayer. Buy or borrow one of the many excellent videos to help set the mood for prayer, like those in the resource list in the back of this prayer guide. Perhaps a large world map or colourful flags would help. If you know people who have travelled widely, consider borrowing souvenirs from them which help people see or feel a foreign culture.

Perhaps you can think of a symbol which will help illustrate prayer. To depict that prayer helps break through spiritual darkness in the 10/40 Window, one church set up a large map with black paper over each of the 10/40 Window countries. Each time they prayed, they removed one of the black coverings to reveal the colourful country underneath.

Pray Out of the Church Building

Another great way to bring prayer to life is to schedule a *prayer-walk*. You might prayer-walk in your own neighbourhood, knowing and remembering others who are prayer-walking among unreached peoples in the 10/40 Window. Maybe your neighbourhood even has a few people who have immigrated from countries of the 10/40 Window. Another idea is to set up stations around your church or home. Each station could have a map, photo, or prayer guide for a different people group in the 10/40 Window. Your prayer team can be divided into groups that can take 10 minutes at each station.

Taste of the Goodness of the Lord

Food is another great way to help people participate. Try planning visits to ethnic restaurants to coincide with your prayer schedule. International cookbooks may also have recipes from specific ethnic groups.

Hear the Call

One church who sponsored a missionary in the 10/40 Window planned a phone call on a Sunday morning to that missionary. They connected the phone call into the church sound system so the whole congregation could hear praise reports and prayer concerns live from the field. After that, they were really ready to pray! If you have trouble finding a missionary to call, consider checking with your denomination or ask for friends of friends who might help. If nothing else, send a team to a local library to look in newspapers and magazines for recent news about an unreached people group. It might even be possible for someone to search for them on the Internet.

Pray Without Ceasing

Special prayer meetings help add variety to the prayer menu. Twenty-four-hour prayer chains or all-night prayer vigils, sometimes in combination with publicly declared fast times, can be well received. If not fasting, potlucks or prayer feasts might spark interest.

Give Everyone a Part

Another church put together a reverse offering. Instead of passing the plate for people to put something in, they passed the plate with slips of paper. Each slip had the name of a people group and each person took a slip as the plate was passed around. Then the each person prayed for the people group they picked up. That way no people group is left out.

Share the Load

Just because there are three or four profiles every day, do not feel like you have to pray for every one. Remember that you are part of millions of people around the globe, lifting these peoples up to the Father. You might try spreading out the prayer. For instance, you could pray for one group in the morning, one at noon, one with the evening meal, and one before bed. Or a small group of people could divide the prayer burden, so every profile gets prayed through, but each person only is responsible for praying for one group in a day. Do not be discouraged if you miss some or fall short of your schedule. Be encouraged that you can join with the whole body of Christ praying for the unreached.

A Word About What Follows...

In the following pages there are 129 prayer profiles for unreached groups across the 10/40 Window. These 129 groups were chosen as representatives of the 1,739 *Joshua Project* peoples. (You can find a complete list in the back of this book.) The profiles may be for individual tribes or people groups, broader language groups, caste or professional groups, or even larger clusters of ethnic groups. In each case we tried to chose a representative photo, but our choices were limited. Almost every page has a map which should help you understand where members of these groups live. However, the maps only show a single location, while most of the groups live in many regions.

We have made every effort to make each profile as complete and up-to-date as time and space allowed, but information will continue to come in for these groups. If you would like to send us a correction or receive more information about a specific group, please contact us at *Caleb Project* or visit our site on the World Wide Web. (See the resource list for addresses.)

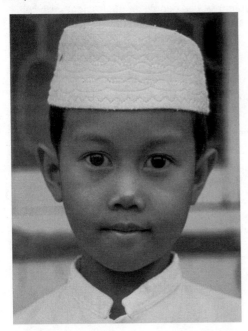

Malay

Homeland: Malaysia, Indonesia,
South Thailand
Religion: Islam, Animism

Azri knelt to wash his hands and feet in preparation for the evening prayers at the *surau* near his home. The cool water running across his skin felt good after a hot day overseeing construction at one of the new high-rise buildings in the city. Azri worked long hours at his job to make certain that his family was well cared for. While a part of him longed for the quiet life he remembered as a boy growing up in the *kampung* (village) of his grandparents, he enjoyed the extra money that his job provided.

Most of Azri's friends from college days had long-ago given up praying five times a day so that they could work longer hours. Azri considered doing the same. He wanted his family to see him as a good Muslim, but had not seen any real benefit from Islam. Knowing that such thoughts would bring sharp criticism, he quickly finished washing and went to pray.

Spread throughout Southeast Asia, the 24 million Muslim Malay are a strong force for Islam in a region most often associated with Buddhism and Animism. Most Malays live in countries whose governments are extremely hostile to any attempts to expose them to Christianity. The handful of Malays who have trusted their lives to Christ now face significant social persecution.

Like Azri, many Malay Muslims stand at a crossroad. Islam has gripped their hearts for nearly seven centuries, but tremendous economic growth and the onslaught of materialism push Malays to the forefront of a struggle. How will they take Islam into the 21st century?

I revealed myself to those who did not ask for me; I was found by those who did not seek me. To a nation that did not call on my name, I said, "Here am I, here am I." Isaiah 65:1

+ More than 15,000 Malays are studying in universities in the United States, England, and Australia. Ask God to raise up individuals and families to befriend these students for the sake of Christ.

+ Pray for Christians in Southeast Asia to grow in their burden for their Malay neighbours and co-workers.

+ Pray that the economic growth in the region might lead to greater openness and opportunities for those who desire to work among the Malay.

+ Pray to remove government restrictions throughout the region which strictly prohibit Malay-focused evangelism.

+ Ask God to strengthen and protect persecuted Malay believers and raise up dynamic Malay Christian leaders.

Acehnese

Homeland: Sumatra, Indonesia
Religion: Islam

Once considered the "gateway to Mecca," Aceh Province (pronounced AH-chay) in Indonesia is home to over three million staunch followers of Islam, the Acehnese. Muslim pilgrims from throughout Indonesia once gathered here at the northern tip of Sumatra to depart for the annual pilgrimage to Mecca, the *Hajj*. The Acehnese have held to Islam more tenaciously than perhaps any other people in Southeast Asia. The Indonesian government designates Aceh as a special province and gives it greater autonomy than other parts of the country. While some Acehnese still dream of building an independent Islamic nation, government troops stand ready to stop any move in that direction. Conversion from Islam is also considered divisive. The Aceh suspect foreigners of being spies, making it difficult for them to work among the Acehnese.

Word of life, as Achenese read their newly available New Testament open their eyes, convict of sin, and bring them to yourself.

Minangkabau

Homeland: Indonesia, Malaysia
Religion: Islam

The 7.5 million Minangkabau, also known as Minang, are one of the most influential Muslim peoples in Indonesia. The largest number live on the west side of the island of Sumatra, though nearly half are scattered throughout Indonesia and Malaysia. Land is inherited through the female line; many Minangkabau men leave their families and villages to make their fortune in other parts of Indonesia or Malaysia. Many of Indonesia's political, business, and religious leaders are Minangkabau men. Because of their success and prestige, planting churches among the Minangkabau may be strategic in reaching Indonesia's hundreds of people groups.

Jesus, draw many Minangkabau men and women to follow you, leading their families and communities into your kingdom.

Komering

Homeland: Sumatra, Indonesia
Religion: Islam, Animism

The majority of the 1.5 million Komering live in the southern region of the island of Sumatra and are bound by a blend of Islam coupled with a deep fear of evil spirits. Closely related to the two million Lampungese also in south Sumatra, the Komering are one of the least-evangelised peoples in the world. The Komering have a reputation for violence; fear of the Komering hinders Indonesian Christians from working among them.

Spirit, stir concern and boldness among Indonesian Christians to serve as your ambassadors among the Komering.

Rejang

Homeland: Sumatra, Indonesia
Religion: Islam

Living in the dense jungles of western Sumatra, the one million Rejang of Bengkulu Province have had little contact with the gospel. Once their culture included human sacrifice and head-hunting, but today they are better known for their wood carving, metal working, and leather and paper plaiting. More than 80 percent live in rural areas.

Father, as your children are forced to move from crowded Java to areas where Rejang live, open doors for them to share their faith with the Rejang.

Sundanese

Homeland: West Java, Indonesia
Religion: Islam

"I believe we can win the Sundanese," said Hamid, a 16th century Muslim leader. He was right. Muslim missionaries successfully converted many Sundanese by communicating the teachings of Islam in culturally relevant ways. Today almost all Sundanese are Muslims, among the staunchest in Indonesia. Less than one tenth of one percent are Christians. The 31 million Sundanese are now considered one of the world's largest unreached people groups.

The Dutch traders who came to Indonesia professed to be Christian, but they placed greater emphasis on business and profit than on sharing the gospel. Some actually hin-dered the work of evangelism in order to preserve peace and commerce. Islam became a rallying point as Muslims fought the influence of these white men from foreign lands.

Early Christian missionaries laboured faithfully among the Sundanese, but failed to pay attention to the Sundanese culture. This resulted in the Sundanese viewing the gospel as European, and the converts to Christianity as people who reject Sundanese ways.

While the Sundanese are Muslim, their religious system is flavoured by Animist, Buddhist, and Hindu rituals passed down from one generation to the next. Special ceremonies mark the birth of a child, its first steps, circumcision, marriage, and burial. These rituals address the life beyond as well. Sundanese respect the powers of the dead and pay homage to unseen spectators. Haunted by spirits from the tops of trees or behind graves, they appeal to their ancestors for help and intercession in times of trouble.

All the nations you have made will come and worship before you, O Lord; they will bring glory to your name. Psalm 86:9

• Pray that God would break Islam's hold on the minds of the people, and that more Muslims leaders would submit to God through his son Jesus.

• Pray that the Lord of the Harvest would send out more workers to do evangelism and church-planting among Sundanese in culturally sensitive ways.

• Although Indonesia is a predominantly Muslim country, the government officially protects freedom of religion. Pray that authorities would not bow to Muslim pressure to further hinder the spread of the gospel.

• West Java has large urban centres, but about 80 percent of the population live in villages. Pray for the rapid spread of the gospel in rural areas.

• Praise God for the witness of a Christian magazine among the Sundanese, one of few magazines of any kind available in the Sundanese language. Pray for the printing and distribution of more Bibles and other Christian literature in Sundanese.

Madurese

Homeland: East Java, Indonesia
Religion: Islam

As one of the four largest peoples in this Muslim nation, the 12 million Madurese are key to seeing God's kingdom established in Southeast Asia. The majority of the Madurese have migrated to the eastern part of the island of Java in search of a more prosperous lifestyle. Those who remain on the island of Madura protect their traditional way of life from modernity and secularism. Other Indonesians say, "If a Madurese is your enemy, you are in trouble, but if a Madurese is your friend, he is your friend for life." Nearly 100 percent of the Madurese are Muslim. Many live in small villages, where they are strongly loyal to *uluma*, religious leaders with mystical powers. The few Madurese who have embraced Christ often must seek refuge from angered family members. However, recent reports say that the young Madurese men are more willing to hear the gospel now than ever.

Father, we pray that your Holy Spirit would soon draw many of these young men to call on Jesus as Saviour and Lord.

Balinese

Homeland: Bali,
Indonesia
Religion: Hinduism

Bali is a Hindu island in the predominantly Muslim nation of Indonesia. Resplendent with natural beauty, the island draws more than a million tourists each year. Thousands of Westerners flood Bali's Kuta Beach but never venture inland to find Bali's soul in the shadow of its holy mountain. Balinese culture is held together by a sense of collective responsibility structured around intricate rituals. Beneath the lush emerald foliage and brilliant tropical flowers the Balinese give themselves to gods and ancestors through beautiful but demonic ceremonies. It is difficult for Balinese to follow Jesus because of the ostracism and persecution this would cause. Less than one percent of the 3.8 million Balinese are Christian. The whole Bible was published in Balinese in 1990.

Lord of the creation, we pray that you might redeem the richness and creativity of Balinese culture and use it to bring glory to your name.

Sasak

Homeland: Lombok, Indonesia
Religion: Islam, Animism

Sasak society is woven around religion—or, more precisely, religions. The Sasak have been affected by Islam, Hinduism, and a unique animistic religion called Wektu Tulu which is practised only on Lombok island, the Sasak homeland. A group called the Wektu Lima Sasak adhere to the more orthodox beliefs and rituals of Islam. *Lima* means "five," and refers to a the five pillars of Islam which believers must follow. In contrast, Wektu Telu Sasaks keep only the first tenet of Islam; that is, the belief in Allah and that Mohammed is his prophet. They pray in their own language and whenever they choose, composing their own prayers in their hearts. Instead of building mosques they designate prayer corners or small rooms facing Mecca in all of their public buildings. Unlike the orthodox, Wektu Telu Sasaks eat pork; they consider everything that comes from Allah to be good.

God of the Sasaks, reveal your son to the Sasak in powerful ways that they might worship you in spirit and in truth.

Buginese

Homeland: Sulawesi, Indonesia
Religion: Islam

The delicious aroma of broiling fish and the happy confusion of children's voices fill the air. On the deck of a wooden sailing vessel, Buginese sailors celebrate their departure on an annual inter-island trading trek.

The seafaring Buginese people naturally prosper in a nation of 13,000 islands. For generations, Buginese men have taken their livelihood from the sea as fishermen, traders, and sometimes pirates. Some Buginese grow rice on irrigated fields further inland, or drive taxis and engage in business in Irian Jaya, another of Indonesia's islands. Many Buginese families' incomes come from the beautiful silk *sarongs* women weave.

Almost all Buginese, also known as the Bugis, adhere to Sunni Islam, a central part of their identity since the 17th century. In addition to Islam, Buginese religion includes offerings to ancestor spirits and a host of other deities.

The Buginese dominate the south western peninsula of Indonesia's Sulawesi Island. They place a high value on status and prestige and view themselves as superior to other ethnic groups. A reputation for arrogance and excellent business skills make the Buginese unpopular with their neighbours.

In spite of their fearsome reputation, outside groups are attempting to win the heart of the Buginese. Islamic organisations would like to establish Muslim learning institutes to teach the Buginese a purer form of Islam. Christian missionaries translated the Bible into the Buginese language in 1900 and finished a revision in 1987. The gospel also comes to the Buginese through daily radio broadcasts.

Yet fewer than a thousand of the four million Buginese have become Christians. The Buginese have little respect for outsiders and are unwilling to receive the gospel from neighbouring people groups like the Toraja. Yet the Buginese are people precious to God. What will shake their pride and allow them to hear of his love?

The smoke of the incense, together with the prayers of the saints, went up before God from the angel's hand. Then the angel took the censer, filled it with fire from the altar, and hurled it on the earth; and there came peals of thunder, rumblings, flashes of lightning and an earthquake. Revelation 8:4-5

• Pray that the Holy Spirit might open up the hearts of the Buginese people to know him. Pray that God would show them his mercy.

• Pray that the Buginese might be fascinated with the Bible translation and the radio broadcasts in their language.

• Pray that the Lord might raise up people whom the Buginese respect to take the gospel to them.

• Pray for the development of strong Buginese churches which would use their language and identify with their culture.

Banjar

Homeland: Kalimantan, Indonesia
Religion: Islam, Animism

Many of the three million Banjar people live along the rivers of southern Kalimantan, Borneo, earning themselves the nickname, "The Water People." Others live in Sumatra Island and Malaysia. The Banjar were Hindu until the 14th century when their Sultan ordered them to turn to Islam. Strong Muslims today, only a handful of Banjar people know Christ. The province of South Kalimantan has many churches, but the Banjar look down on other ethnic groups. Although they do not respect local believers, the Banjar respect foreign Christians from developed countries. However, for the last three years Christian workers have gathered weekly to pray for the Banjar people and recently a Banjar became an evangelist.

Father, use your children from afar to reach out to the Banjarese, and raise up evangelists so all Banjarese would have a chance to know you.

Gorontolo

Homeland: Indonesia
Religion: Islam

When he heard the noon-time call to prayer, Gagah knelt reverently on his prayer rug with his face to the ground. As he recited the words of the prayer, he begged Allah for a good job. Gahah lives by growing cloves and rice for the city market. The 800,000 Gorontalo scattered throughout north Sulawesi have little interest in other cultures. Because they speak no trade language, the Gorontolo cannot find good jobs and retreat further into their own societies. At one time they were strongly oriented toward the sea; a life of trade exposed them to outside ways and ideas, including the acceptance of Islam from 16th century Arab traders. However mission work recently began among the Gorontolo.

China
Banjar
Muslims-Magindanaw (Ilanum)
Gorontalo
Makassarese
Buginese
Australia

Lord, use the radio broadcasts, Bible cassettes, and culturally-sensitive mission efforts so the Gorontolo would seek after the one true God.

Makassarese

Homeland: Indonesia
Religion: Islam

Sitting on a ridge above his parents' small rice farm on Sulawesi Island, overlooking the Java Sea, Ibraham could see flocks of gulls darting toward the fishing boats to steal fresh fish. How good it was to be home for a few days from the university! As a faithful Muslim, Ibrahim supplemented his courses at technical school with Islamic studies at one of the city's mosques. Studying the history of his people, he learned that when Javanese and Malay merchants preached Islam to the Makassarese 300 years ago, they accepted it because their own religion was based on the principle of *tauhid*, belief in one God.

Jesus, work among Makassarese students, challenging their hearts with Christ's claims as Son of the one true God.

Muslims of the Philippines

The 13 million Muslims of the southern Philippines have a long history of grievances against Christians. Spaniards colonising the Philippines persecuted the Muslims for not accepting Catholicism. When the Philippines came under United States control, large corporations took over vast tracks of Muslim land and used northern, Catholic farmers to work the land. When the Philippines became independent, Muslims still suffered and committed brutal acts of violence against Catholic Filipinos who lived among them. Many Filipino Muslims see Christians as enemies. When will it end?

Spirit, please bring about repentance and reconciliation in this bloody conflict.

Khmer

Homeland: Cambodia
Religion: Buddhism, Atheism

Photo Courtesy Kevin Morris for OMF International.

Imagine yourself a Khmer teenager in Cambodia. The ravages of war, genocide, and poverty have decimated the older generations, so you and your peers constitute over half of the country's population. Communist ideas still linger in the school system, so you have learned little about God or Cambodia's national religion, Buddhism. In the early 1990's, some degree of democracy and freedom were restored and brought new hope to your country. However, freedom has opened the door to a growing drug trade. Cambodia has become a distribution hub for heroin and opium. Chinese from mainland China run drug mafias, often collaborating with government officials. Despite their destructive effects, drugs tempt you by falsely promising euphoria and wealth.

Another growing scourge is child prostitution. The alarming spread of disease among prostitutes fuels the demand for more prostitutes. Young girls are often kidnapped, sold, and ultimately enslaved into the flesh trade. The immorality rampant in Khmer culture may be traced back to the religious practices of Khmer kings in the 12th-15th centuries, who, according to tradition, believed they could gain strength by having relations with evil spirits. Young Khmer are constantly bombarded by seductive media images and peer pressure. If this were not enough, the Khmer Rouge ("Red Khmer"), which killed millions in the mid-1970's, continues to threaten the fragile and corrupt democratic government.

But, there is hope. Since Communism collapsed, freedom of religion has been restored. The open practice of Buddhism has returned and interest is growing among your countrymen.

Your soul is hungry too, but the traditions of Buddhism can seem fearful, empty, ritualistic, and superstitious. Recently you went with a friend to see the *Jesus* film and you are now curious about this strange religion. Who is this man, Jesus?

Come to me, all you who are weary and burdened, and I will give you rest. Matthew 11:28

• Pray that this generation of Khmer youth would turn to Christ in large numbers.

• Pray for the Khmer church. Less than one percent of Khmer people are evangelical Christians. Young believers suffer from the lack of follow-up and leadership training, and the disunity among Christians. Pray for forgiveness and reconciliation to prevail.

• Pray against the tide of drug addiction and sexual immorality that infects the culture, especially the younger generation.

• Pray that the light of the gospel would shine in the spiritual shadows of the Khmer culture. Fear associated with ubiquitous spirit shrines and the hatred from 20 years of war need to be replaced with love.

Bouyei

Homeland: China, Burma
Religion: Animism

Visiting a Bouyei home, you see spells written on thin paper fluttering over the windows. Above the door, a mirror hangs to reflect demons away. Across the room stand five altars to the gods of sky, earth, ancestor, country, and education. With a population between two and three million, the Bouyei are one of China's largest minorities. The largest concentration lives in the Yunnan plateau of south west China. Most are farmers. A few Bouyei are believers, but most have never even heard of Jesus.

Lord of the harvest, mobilise the growing church among the neighbouring Hmong people to reach out cross-culturally to the unreached Bouyei.

Lao

Homeland: Laos, Cambodia, Vietnam
Religion: Buddhism, Animism

A small wooden raft laden with candles is gently slipped into the Mekong River. It hesitates, then catches the current and joins many similar rafts bobbing in the murky water. This scapegoat raft carryies the year's guilt and trouble as it floats away. Unlike other Asian communist countries, Laos remains devoted to Buddhism. In Laos, unlike Vietnam and China, monks are seen everywhere. The Lao blend their Buddhism with Animism, practising sorcery and protecting themselves from evil spirits. They seek merit through good behaviour, ritual sacrifices, reverence for religious images, and offerings to the monks. Less than one percent of the Lao in Laos are evangelical Christians.

Lamb of God, give Lao believers and missionaries spiritual wisdom and cultural insight to use analogies like the "scapegoat raft" to communicate the gospel to the Lao.

Li

Homeland: China
Religion: Animism

Off the southern coast of China lies the large island of Hainan, home to more than one million Li people. Generations of Chinese have viewed Hainan as backward and undesirable. When former Chinese prime minister Li Deyu was exiled to Hainan during the Tang Dynasty (618-907 AD), he described it as "the gate to hell." In the last decade, however, local officials have worked to turn the island into an exotic resort destination. Historically, the Li people practised Animism, turning to shamans, witches, and animal sacrifice. Recently, the Li have abandoned traditional culture and embraced modern living. Traditional costumes are put away except for tourist performances and funeral ceremonies. There are a few small Li churches, but most Li have never heard anything about Jesus Christ.

Lord, burden believing Chinese tourists to Hainan with a vision to return and evangelise the Li.

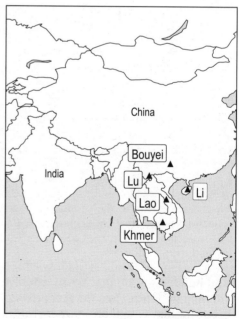

Photo Courtesy Jack Hollingsworth for OMF International.

Thai

Homeland: Thailand
Religion: Buddhism

In the earliest moments of the morning the sun glistens on the gaudy golden spikes of the Buddhist monasteries. With the roosters' crow, bald monks wrapped in saffron robes glide through the streets and beg for breakfast. Temples, monasteries, shrines, and spirit houses are the anchors of Thai culture and the backdrop for this long-standing morning routine.

Spirit houses stand in front of every farmhouse in central Thailand, along rough passages of road in the south, and even on the sidewalk outside the McDonald's in Bangkok. The Thai way of sheltering the spirits of the property, these houses range in style from miniature temples to simple covered boxes. Thai routinely leave offerings of food and other provisions to keep these spirits as comfortable as possible, hoping the spirits will return their kindness.

At the same time, many of today's Thai are drawn to the gods of materialism and independence, trends that are changing the face of east Asia. Traffic is one of the greatest problems in Bangkok: each day, more than a thousand new cars crowd already overcrowded streets. The Thai, however, face such difficulties with good humour and innovation. Traffic cops dance in the intersections to amuse and ease tense drivers; families eat around the dashboard instead of the dining room table.

A problem more difficult to adjust to is the public health crisis brought on by the spread of sexually transmitted disease. Bangkok, sometimes called the "sin capital" of Asia, is home to a sex industry employing two million people, including many children. AIDS and the orphans it will leave is one of the country's greatest concerns. The government projects that four million people in Thailand will be infected with HIV in the next four years.

And he died for all, that those who live should no longer live for themselves but for him who died for them and was raised again. 2 Corinthians 5:15

• Missionaries have been working in Thailand for many years, but only one percent of the Thai have accepted Jesus. Many Thai find it hard to understand the concept of grace and forgiveness. Pray that the Holy Spirit would give them understanding.

• Pray for the victims of the sex industry in Bangkok, many of whom are children. The fear of AIDS has caused many government leaders to rethink the current entertainment industry and are beginning to enforce positive changes.

• Pray that Christians around the world would take advantage of the opportunity to share Christ in Thailand, where there are few restrictions on ministry.

• Even in rural Thailand literacy is on the rise. Pray that many would take advantage of the Christian and evangelistic literature that could explain Jesus to them.

• Pray for the young Christians in Thailand who have few role models in extremely sinful surroundings.

Shan

Homeland: Myanmar, China, Thailand
Religion: Buddhism

Shan simply means "mountain" and is used to describe several Asian mountain peoples. The Burmese Shan are part of the Tai family and consider themselves the older, wiser brothers of the Thai and Lao people. Traditionally, the Shan live in bamboo homes high in the mountains, but in recent years many Shan have travelled to Thailand to find work. The Shan faithfully follow magic rituals, horoscopes, and dreams. They carefully tend their spirit houses, believing they only worship good spirits, mixing Buddhist tradition with magic. Most Shan boys join the Buddhist priesthood for a year or two when they are about ten years old. Scriptures have been available for the Shan since 1892. Some Shan have come to Christ through radio broadcasts, literature, the hard work of missionaries, and a new translation of the New Testament. Pockets of believers around the world have been praying specifically for large numbers of Shan to come to Christ. Will you join them?

Holy Spirit, work especially among young families, who have been noticeably absent from the small Shan churches.

Zhuang

Homeland: Southwestern China
Religion: Buddhism, Animism

The Zhuang live along the terraced, narrow mountains of Guangxi, Yunnan, Guangdong, Guiahou, and Hunan Provinces in China. A very musical people, the Zhuang have made impromptu singing an art form and use it for courtship, settling disputes, and in celebrations and community festivals. Many are wet-rice farmers, but they also grow bananas, pineapple, timber, and cultured pearls. They live Thai-style, in two-story homes: the family lives upstairs and the downstairs is used to store equipment and animals. The 16 million Zhuang are the largest minority group in China. There are a few Christians among them, about one Christian for every thousand Zhuang.

Father, use radio, the Jesus film, and the New Testament in translation, emboldening Zhuang believers to win many to you.

Black Tai

Homeland: Vietnam, China, Laos
Religion: Animism

The Black Tai, or Tai Dam, live on the banks of the Black River in Vietnam. One of the few Tai groups not influenced by Buddhism, the Black Tai hold tightly to centuries-old, never-ending rituals to keep the spirit world happy. In the last several years God has been moving among the Black Tai in Vietnam. A few years ago one Black Tai in prison received Christ. Once released, he began sharing Christ with his neighbours. Before long, more than 750 Black Tai had come to Christ. Since then, the church has been growing quickly. Entire villages have converted. Thousands have come to Christ and Bibles in the Black Tai language are being distributed.

Jesus, teach these young believers so they can stay strong in a country where persecution of your children is on the rise.

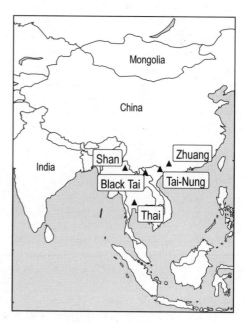

Photo Courtesy Jack Hollingsworth for OMF International.

Hui

Homeland: China
Religion: Islam

China's ancient capital, Xian was the beginning of the ancient Silk Road, the city of eternal peace. Tourists flock to see thousands of life-size statues of soldiers and horses, the terra-cotta army of a dead emperor. In the background, a call to prayer rises from the Great Mosque, the largest centre of Muslim worship in all of China. Also in this city, a stone tablet from 781 AD commemorates the first Christian mission to China.

Christianity and Islam both came to China in the 7th century: Arabs brought Islam here, along the famous "Silk Road" and southern sea trade routes; Syrians brought Christianity, crossing Central Asian deserts to bring goods to the emperor's court. Legend has it that T'ai Tsung, China's greatest emperor, had a dream about a turbaned man who chased away demons. His advisors identified this man as a Muslim, and counselled T'ai Tsung to allow Islam into China in order to chase away demons plaguing their land.

Islam penetrated China's interior during the next two centuries. Today ten of China's 55 official ethnic minorities are Muslim. The nearly nine million Hui are the largest of these Muslim groups. Some Hui are descendants of Muslim men who married Chinese women, while others are recent converts to Islam. They speak the Mandarin Chinese language with some borrowed Arabic and Persian words. What sets them apart is their Muslim religion. Hui men wear a round white cap to distinguish themselves as Muslims, and they refuse to eat pork, drink alcohol, or engage in gambling. Many younger Hui practice Islam only nominally but continue to resist assimilation into Han culture. Close-knit Hui communities centre around restaurants and mosques and the leadership of powerful religious leaders.

The Hui are respected for their contributions to science, warfare, and literature. Hui communities are found throughout China, especially in Ningxia, Yunnan, Xinjiang, and Gansu provinces and Beijing. There is little or no Christian witness to the Hui people of China. However God is beginning to call missionaries to go the Hui. Many of these are Chinese Christians from other countries. Radio broadcasts with special programs tailored to Muslim audiences have targeted these people loved by God.

If you belong to Christ, then you are Abraham's seed, and heirs according to the promise.
Galatians 3:29

⬧ Ask the Lord to break down spiritual strongholds and release the Hui from oppression into the kingdom of his Son.

⬧ Pray that doors would open for ministry among the Hui through trade, cultural exchanges, and educational opportunities.

⬧ Pray that the Hui would see their righteousness as "filthy rags," their good works as insufficient for salvation. May they turn to Christ for the forgiveness of sins.

⬧ Thank God for the move of his Spirit and the growth of churches among other Chinese peoples, such as the 80 million Han, in China and on every continent of the world. Pray that the Lord would raise up from among them labourers for his harvest.

Japanese

Homeland: Japan
Religion: Shintoism, Buddhism

At rush hour in Tokyo, subway guards wearing white gloves pack commuters into the cars like sardines in a can. Under the serene majesty of Mt. Fuji live 15 million people in the urban sprawl of Tokyo, Yokohama, and Kawasaki. Another major urban strip packs 12 million people between Osaka and Kobe. The Japanese total 126 million. Cramped in cities, constricted by mountains, isolated by oceans, the Japanese present a unified culture that rivals the major economic powers of the world. Recent events have threatened some of that unity and stability, including a devastating earthquake in Kobe and a subway poison gas attack by the Aum Shinrikyo cult. Growing unemployment, economic recession, high-stress lifestyles, moral decline, and youthful rebellions against authority have left many Japanese disillusioned. Will the Shinto-Buddhist beliefs carry the Japanese through these trials? Despite many years of Western and Korean Christian presence, few Japanese have received Jesus as Lord and Saviour.

Holy Spirit, open Japanese eyes to see Christ not as a foreign god, but the Saviour of the world.

Tujia

Homeland: China
Religion: Taoism,
        Animism, Atheism

Rice paddies contour the terraced mountainsides; in the green valleys below, wheat, maize, potatoes, and tea trace colourful geometric patterns. Almost six million Tujia live in the semi-tropical forests of China's Hunan and Hubei provinces. A few in isolated areas still speak the Tujia language, but most are learning the languages of dominant cultures.

The Tujia use song and dance to tell epic sagas and creation myths, expressing love and grief with the movement of their hands. Their embroidery, weaving, and quilting are objects of art. Ninety percent of the 1,000 students at Western Hebei University are Tujia. Might this be a door of opportunity for Christian teachers?

Lord of creation, redeem the Tujia festivals, so Tujia would know the joy of Christ and express their love for you through their dance and creative energy.

Yao

Homeland: Vietnam, China
Religion: Animism, Atheism

During spring planting, 20 or 30 Yao families gather together to plough and sow each other's fields. A young man stands in the field beating a drum and leading the workers in song. As with the Tujia, singing is a focus of Yao society. The Yao are skilled weavers and specialise in embroidered indigo cloth. Several people groups are included in the 2.7 million Yao, speaking different dialects and spread across the Asian continent. About half speak dialects of their own Chinese-Tibetan language, while the rest have adopted the languages of surrounding peoples. Traditionally farmers and hunters, their staple diet consists of tea leaves fried in oil and boiled into a thick, salty soup with puffed rice or soybeans. The Yao worship their ancestors as well as many gods, although atheistic communism has eroded much of their belief system. However, as many as 9,000 Yao know Jesus, although translation of a Yao Bible is incomplete.

Jesus, may every Yao village have a church which worships and glorifies you.

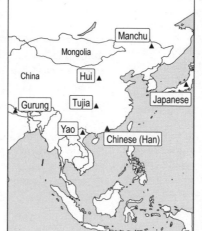

Tibetans

Homeland: China, Tibet, Nepal
Religion: Tibetan Buddhism

Photo Courtesy Jack Hollingsworth for OMF International.

Tashi, an Amdo Tibetan, braced himself for another frigid blast of wind and sleet while trying to guide his half-frozen yaks to a large, sheltering rock. He thought, "I wish I were back in the tent with my wife Dolma and the children, sipping hot yak butter tea. But if I don't care for the yak, soon there will be no food for us."

Tashi and his family are nomads on the rich grasslands of eastern Qinghai Province. Their herds graze in a dramatic landscape including vast Qinghai lake, rippling grasses, high mountains, and alkali flatlands. Some of his fellow Amdo-speaking Tibetans are farmers growing barley and other crops. While few of the six million Tibetans have heard the life-giving gospel, even fewer of the nearly one million Amdo Tibetans have.

As Tashi pushed toward the shelter, he worried about his leg which was badly injured a month ago. He had asked his cousin, a Tibetan Buddhist monk, to pray for its healing. It felt better for a few days, but then it began to hurt twice as much. Tashi wondered if the doctors in town could help him, but it was so far away.

Instantly, Tashi forgot his pain as he began to worry about the demons which controlled this giant rock. As sleet bit into his face, he cried, "This is a life of suffering; but if I build up enough merit, then I'll have a higher birth in my next life."

Tashi's religion provides him little lasting comfort. Like most Amdo Tibetans and 13 million others, Tashi is a follower of Tibetan Buddhism, an historic blend of several Asian religions with a strong occult aspect. Its followers believe that if they work hard to earn merit, they will escape from the long cycle of life, death, reincarnation, life, death, reincarnation. Bad deeds may lead to being reborn to a "lower state," such as a beggar or animal.

Tibetan Buddhism stresses the concept of detachment from life, in many ways the opposite of the Christian virtue of love.

So if the Son sets you free, you will be free indeed. John 8:36

◆ Less than one percent of the Amdo Tibetans are believers. Pray that Tibetan Christians and other Christians would come to Amdo areas to demonstrate and tell of Jesus' love.

◆ Pray that Christians living among them would know how to share Christ in a way that Tibetan Buddhists could understand and appreciate.

◆ Thank God for the few Christians reaching out to Tibetan peoples with loving help, the New Testament, and Christian broadcasting. Ask the Lord to lead them to those ready to hear and consider salvation.

◆ Most of the six million Tibetans do not know about the church, nor do they have a church in their area. Pray that God would spread healthy, loving, worshipping fellowships among all Tibetans.

Bhutanese

Homeland: Bhutan, Nepal, India
Religion: Buddhism

The Drukpa majority in Bhutan dominate the government and are strongly Buddhist. Few have ever heard the gospel. Most of the believers are isolated and scattered with little opportunity for fellowship, and some have suffered for their faith. The Drukpa include two main groups, the Ngalongs, who speak Dzongkha, and the Sharchops, who speak Sharchagpakha. Parts of the New Testament have been translated into Dzongkha, but are only in draft form. The main translator has died. Bible translation is under way in the Sharchagpakha language.

Father we ask you to establish a vital witnessing fellowship among every ethnic subgroup of the Drukpa. Please bring your word to the hearts of the Bhutanese.

Burmese

Homeland: Myanmar
Religion: Buddhism

There are nearly 30 million ethnically Burmese people in the world, and most live in the strife-ridden country of Myanmar, formerly known as Burma. Tens of thousands of believers live in Myanmar, but most are ethnically Chinese or among the Karen and Kachin minority peoples who have recently experienced a wonderful awakening to the gospel. Drama is the mainstay of Burman popular street-level culture. Performances can recount Buddhist legends or involve slapstick comedy, dance, ensemble singing, or giant puppets, but always include Burman music with drums, harps, gongs, and bamboo flutes. Burmese eat rice often with spicy chilli or *ngapi*, a dried and fermented shrimp paste.

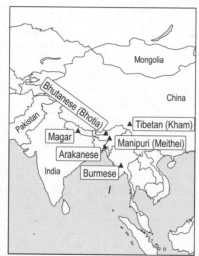

Lord, thank you for pouring out your grace on hidden peoples in Myanmar. Remember also the Buddhist Burmese and teach your church how to use Burmese cultural forms to evangelise.

Arakanese

Homeland: Myanmar, Bangladesh
Religion: Buddhism, Islam

Peace and prosperity have evaded the Arakanese in Myanmar and Bangladesh. Nearly two million Arakanese people live in the high mountainous forests of western Myanmar and are persecuted by the Burmese majority. About half of the Arakanese are Muslims, many of whom have left Myanmar because of persecution. Bangladesh, the second most densely populated nation on earth, has accepted many of these refugees, but the Bengalis also look down on them, believing their ancestors were pirates.

Jesus, you were persecuted and despised by many, please reveal yourself to the Arakanese as the source of peace and security.

Manipuri

Homeland: India
Religion: Hinduism, Islam

Drama, storytelling, and dance are high favorites among the people who live in the Manipuri state of north east India. When the Manipuri Hindus celebrated India Independence Day on August 15, 1994, thousands heard the gospel story for the first time in their own language, Meithei, through the *Jesus* film. The Bible has been translated into Meithei and there are now more than 10,000 Manipuri Christians.

King Jesus, please provide discipleship for believers and those whose lives have been touched by the Jesus film. We pray for wide distribution of your word in Meithei.

Bengali

Homeland: Bangladesh, India
Religion: Islam, Hinduism

Northeast of India lies Bangladesh, "Land of the Bengalis." 125 million Bengalis call Bangladesh home while another roughly 62 million live across the border in the Indian state of West Bengal. The British ruled the area from the 18th century to 1947 when East Bengal became part of Pakistan. Bangladesh declared its independence in 1971 and, in the ensuing civil war, millions died or fled to India.

Islam is the religion of most Bengalis. Muslim invaders conquered the formerly Hindu area in the 12th century. Today 85 percent of Bengalis are Muslim, but the Hindus form a sizeable minority of about 12 percent. Most of the remainder are Buddhists or Christians. Like Muslims in many parts of the world, many Bengalis today believe the tombs of ancient holy men to be places of great spiritual power, and their pre-Islamic belief in *jinn*, or spirits, still controls much of their daily lives.

Because most missionary efforts have been directed toward the Hindu Bengalis who have seemed more receptive to the gospel than Muslims, the Bengali churches that have grown from these efforts have a Hindu flavour, offensive to many Bengali Muslims. Few Bengali Muslims have come to Christ, and most of these have been cut off from their families and communities. In the early 1970's, frustrated missionaries in Bangladesh began to try some new approaches to winning Bengali Muslims. They began to eat, dress, and live as their Muslim neighbours did. They sat in the marketplace as Muslim teachers did, discussing spiritual things. As Bengali Muslims began to convert, they established small congregations formed along Bengali Muslim patterns. Although these congregations are a promising start, most Bengalis still have no opportunity to hear the gospel.

May the peoples praise you, O God; may all the peoples praise you. Psalm 67:3

⬧ Pray that God would break through the spiritual darkness which enshrouds the millions of Bengalis who live in Bangladesh and India. Ask him to free them from their fear of spirits and to give them new life in Christ.

⬧ Ask God to send more missionaries to the Bengalis and to give them wisdom to present the gospel in ways that can be understood and received by the people.

⬧ Pray for the discipleship of Bengali Hindus and Muslims who have converted to Christianity, that they might be unshakeable in their faith, equipped to take the gospel to every sector of Bengali society.

⬧ Poverty, crowding, illiteracy, and devastating storms and floods plague the Bengali people. Ask our merciful God to relieve their suffering.

Assamese

Homeland: Assam, India
Religion: Hinduism, Islam

About 14 million Assamese-speaking people live in north east India, primarily in the state of Assam. Dependent on the land, most Assamese live in rural settings where they grow rice, jute, and tea, and profit from rich mineral resources. Two faults running parallel to the southern Himalayas make their the region vulnerable to earthquakes. Malnutrition is also common, made worse by poor sanitation and contaminated water sources. An artistic and creative people, the Assamese enjoy poetry, literature, and music. Like many Hindus, they accept difficulties without complaining, seeing their lives decreed by fate. The Assamese have simple lives without many material comforts. For many years, Assamese Hindus and Bengali Muslims have been fighting over territorial rights in this area. Christians, who represent only a small fraction of the population, are appreciated for their efforts in relief work and education.

Father, let the compassion and faithfulness of Assamese Christians lead many Hindus and Muslims to a better peace in Christ.

Bihari

Homeland: Nepal, India
Religion: Hinduism, Animism

"Evil spirit, leave my daughter!" the distraught Bhojpuri mother shrieked as she hit the girl on the head with her Bible. She was a new Christian who had not yet learned the power of prayer. Later, one of the few Christians in her village prayed for the little girl in the name of Jesus, and she was healed. Because of this, others in the village also prayed in the name of Jesus. There are nearly 90 million Bihari-speaking Bhojpuris in India and Nepal, making them one of the largest unreached people groups in the world. Yet those who profess Christ are zealous for the gospel. One missionary worked with Bhojpuri people with little response. Then he met an illiterate Bhojpuri believer. He helped him learn to read, and the two men went to seven villages where there were tiny Christian groups. They trained one person in each village to share the gospel and went on to other villages and trained new believers in the same way.

Dear Lord, please use these two men along with many others to plant dynamic, growing churches in every Bhojpuri village. Help the Bhojpuri to understand the power of prayer.

Oriya

Homeland: Orissa, India
Religion: Hinduism

Roughly 33 million Indians speak the Oriya language which was derived from ancient Sanskrit. They live primarily in the Indian state of Orissa. The first convert of early 19th century missionaries to Orissa was a high caste Brahmin. Within a few years the number of believers had grown to 20, all from the highest castes. Believing that the best way to reach more Oriyas was to send Oriya evangelists, the missionaries had trained and ordained 15 Oriya Christians by 1840. But as more Oriyas became Christians, they began living in exclusively Christian communities. As a result, relatively few of the Oriya people throughout India are now evangelical Christians. Today missionaries and Christians from a tribal background are persecuted in Orissa.

Holy Spirit, raise up Indian missionaries who can see and cross the barriers of language and culture to reach Oriyas.

Hindi-Speaking Hindus

Homeland: India
Religion: Hinduism

A mother stands waist-deep in the holy Ganges river, cradling her first-born son in her arms. Tears stream down her face as she thinks about what she is going to do. She must appease the gods so that her husband will be able to find work. She must atone for her own sins. Offering her son as a sacrifice is the only way she knows to make atonement; lesser sacrifices of food and small animals have brought no results. She takes a deep breath and gently puts him under the filthy water.

In India, home to nearly a billion people, 800 million people speak the Hindi language. The majority of them also follow the Hindu religion and are born into a *caste* structure which will dictate much of their life.

Several miles away a small procession winds down the street. Seven Hindu boys are being led to a temple to be offered as sacrifices to the goddess Devi. Decades ago one of them would have been slaughtered. Today a goat will replace the human sacrifice. Yet other children are sold into slavery as temple prostitutes. Many of them will not survive the torture, drug addiction, and abuse they will be subjected to before they reach adolescence.

While there has been significant outreach to Hindus for more than a century, the gospel has penetrated mainly the lowest castes or classes. Indian Christians and missionaries are seeking God for breakthroughs in the rest of the population during this decade. Many are reaching out to the millions of children in India, who are perhaps the most literate, well-educated generation India has ever known. Might God raise up Josiahs, Timothys, and Davids from this young generation of Hindus?

For I desire mercy, not sacrifice, and acknowledgment of God rather than burnt offerings. Hosea 6:6

• Pray for freedom and release for Hindi-speaking families who offer their children to the gods in desperation. Ask God to reveal himself as the only perfect sacrifice for sins.

• Ask God to provide employment for adults who want to work, but cannot find a job. Pray for creative ways to help these impoverished Hindus.

• Praise God that committed Hindu groups are showing increased interest in the gospel. Pray for success of upcoming evangelistic events. Also pray that high caste Hindus would continue to come to Christ in increasing numbers.

• Pray that the Hindu festivals celebrating the triumph of good over evil would provide many opportunities for Christians to explain the good news of the gospel.

• Ask God to protect the lives of Hindu converts who face much opposition from family, friends, and employers when they turn to Christ.

Gujarati

Homeland: India, Pakistan
Religion: Hinduism

"Does cousin Deepak live in London?" Pragna asked. "No, it is Dilip who is in London. Deepak is in Dar es Salaam, in Tanzania, Africa." This conversation could take place in almost any family of the Patel caste, part of the approximately 132 million people who speak the Gujarati language. Patels are very business oriented and have found success all over the world. Besides India and Pakistan, Patels are found in Africa, east Asia, Great Britain, and the US. In fact, if you look in your phone book under "Patel" you may find a few living near you.

Lord, seek out your wandering children among the Patels, draw them to yourself and call them to invest in your kingdom where rust does not destroy. Plant a vigorous Gujarati-speaking church everywhere Patels live.

Marathi

Homeland: India
Religion: Hinduism

Most of Maharashtra state's people speak the Marati (pronounced ma-RA-ty) language. This wealthy state is highly industrialized and is home to such world-class cities as Bombay (now called Mumbai) and Puna, making Marati-speaking people some of the most influential in India. The Maratha (ma-RA-ta) caste, one of India's farming castes, is one such influential group. Despite the fact that there is less persecution of Christians in this area, the Maratha have not been exposed much to the gospel in terms that make sense in their culture. There are very few known Maratha believers. At the other end of the spectrum of Marathi-speaking groups are the Animist Mang caste. They make brooms and mats or work as agricultural labourers. While they have gospel cassettes, radio programmes, and the *Jesus* film all in their language, there are as few as 1,200 Christians, less than 0.07 percent of the 1.8 million Mang.

King Jesus, call Marathi-speaking people to come to you and forsake everything for you.

Gujjar

Homeland: India, Pakistan, Afghanistan
Religion: Islam, Animism, Hinduism

Gujjar life is shaped by the seasons. Traditionally nomadic, the Gujjar spend each winter in the low-lying plains. Once spring comes, they climb higher and higher into the Himalayan mountains as ice on the mountain meadows thaws. The Gujjar travel great distances over these snow-bound mountain ranges to bring their cattle, goats, and sheep from one pasture to another. A colourful, spirited, and hope-filled people, the Gujjar nevertheless find their herds, families, and way of life threatened by rising militancy in their traditional Indian state, Jammu and Kashmir. Because they lack education and experience, Gujjar are often taken advantage of in the marketplace.

Father, move your church in compassion to meet Gujjar parents' growing desire for schooling for their children, and bring them news of your peace and mercy.

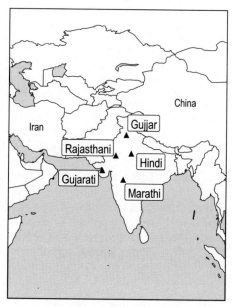

Bhil

Photo Courtesy Jim Myers.

Homeland: India
Religion: Animism, Hinduism

It was a scene witnessed over and over by India's Bhil tribes. A mob of 500 people descended on a woman accused of practising witchcraft and stoned her to death. The eight million Bhils, one of India's ancient tribal groups known as the "first people," worship ancestral spirits as well as Hindu deities. Each village has its own sorcerers who appease the gods through rituals of witchcraft and elaborate sacrifices.

According to Bhil belief, sickness and disease come from the work of evil spirits. Bhil live in great fear of the evil eye. Many people die because they seek ineffective remedies from these sorcerers. Others are killed because of accusations that they misuse their magical powers. Is it any wonder neighbouring peoples consider the Bhil superstitious?

Bhil peoples are scattered across central India, often living in remote, inaccessible parts of Gujarat, Rajasthan, Maharashtra, and Madhya Pradesh. While some have assimilated into mainstream Hindu society, the pride and identity of the Bhil and other indigenous peoples of India has been growing through the *adivasi* or "original people" movement.

The Bhil love and honour their families and tribes, taking their identity from these relationships. They see the boundaries between life and death as permeable. The living feel a sense of connection with their ancient ancestors, and this gives them strength.

Some Bhils in Rajasthan have come to Christ and been delivered from the power of evil spirits, resulting in the baptism of hundreds of witnesses. However, there are only a handful of believers across the central Indian state of Madhya Pradesh.

They exchanged the truth of God for a lie, and worshiped and served created things rather than the Creator—who is forever praised. Romans 1:25

• Pray for the Bhils to recognise the Creator God as the true god.

• Praise God for the new Bhil believers in Rajasthan. Pray for their outreach to other Bhil tribes and villages.

• Ask God to multiply the Christian workers among Bhil and other tribal people. Pray for medical workers who could effectively demonstrate the power of prayer and medicine over disease.

• Pray for God to demonstrate his power in dramatic ways to Bhils who live in the bondage and fear of evil spirits.

• Pray for translation and literacy work recently begun among the Bhil tribes.

Gond

Homeland: India
Religion: Animism

The Maria woman and her daughter spent the day in the forest gathering honey and wild fruit while her husband hunted for winter meat. When they returned to their village, they joined the other villagers gathering to watch a cockfight. Their daughter went off to join the other girls and boys for an evening of games and dances which quickly passed the line into sensuality. Like other Gond tribes, the Maria are animists; the name Maria means "men of the woods." The Maria worship earth gods. In fact, their priests believe that unless clan gods are continuously worshipped, the village will starve. Fewer than a hundred of the 110,000 Maria Gonds are Christians. There are no scriptures or gospel recordings in their language.

Holy God, reveal yourself to the Gond as the creator, far more worthy of worship than anything you created.

Lambadi

Homeland: India
Religion: Animists

The light-skinned Lambadi gypsies of India are a tribal group related to European gypsies. Traditionally nomadic, the Lambadi (also known as Banjara) have been forced to settle down in villages, farming, and construction work. Although they no longer have the freedom their grandparents had, Lambadi protect themselves from entanglements by living in small, isolated groups and shunning contact with other peoples. While some Lambadi are wealthy, others are among the poorest of the poor. Most have very little education and few can read, though some villages have welcomed literacy workers. In spite of their independence and isolation, some Lambadi have come to know Jesus. Recently three fellowship groups were formed. When some of the new believers travelled to a distant village to minister, they found 90 other Lambadi Christians waiting for them!

Lord, establish strong, vital churches among the Lambadi, so they might be used to reach others.

Munda-Santal

Homeland: India
Religion: Hinduism, Animism

Imagine a whole society, including a religion, centred around iron and fire. Such is the life of the Agaria people, one of India's tribal groups. They worship a fire god and an iron demon, *Lohasure*, whom they believe lives in their kilns. The name Agaria is derived from that of a fire god. These iron-smelters and blacksmiths involve their whole families in their trade. Like most of the other tribal people in the large Munda-Santal cluster, the Agaria hold to animistic beliefs and practices overlaid with a veneer of Hinduism. As the Agaria work at their furnaces and kilns each day, they pray that the gods will not fall asleep and leave them without the protection they need to prevent accidents.

Spirit, send labourers to the Agaria who would show them the living, powerful God, not only the God of iron and power but also of mercy and forgiveness. May they know you, the God who never sleeps!

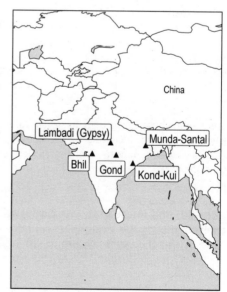

Photo Courtesy John Cornish, CBI.

Sindhi

Homeland: Pakistan, India
Religion: Hinduism, Islam

Sindhi now live in several states and countries, though they get their name and language from the Sindh province of what is now Pakistan. When British colonial empire broke up 50 years ago the Indian subcontinent was divided into Hindu and Muslim countries: India and Pakistan. The Sindhis, who include both Hindus and Muslims, live in both countries. Hindu Sindhis living in Pakistan have been harshly persecuted by the Muslim Sindhi majority.

In both countries, Sindhi-speakers are diverse. One segment of Hindu Sindhi society, the *Bhaibands*, are traders and shop keepers; the backbone of India's middle class. Another, the *Amils*, are civil servants, teachers, and scholars. Among Hindu Sindhis, church-planting efforts have shown some minimal success, perhaps mitigated by the prosperity and materialism of Hindu Sindhi culture.

In Pakistan, 80 percent of the Sindhis are Muslim. The Moguls who ruled this land for nearly 300 years left Islam firmly entrenched. While there is a Christian presence in Sindh Province and believers scattered throughout the districts, most are Punjabis or come from the Hindu Sindhi groups. The Muslim Sindhis, and especially those who live in the countryside, have very little opportunity to hear the gospel and fewer than 50 have embraced the gospel. Nevertheless, in the cities mission hospitals and Bible correspondence courses provide a Christian presence.

Many Sindhis have taken their business skills to other parts of the world, including Africa, Europe, and the U.S., where they can more easily be reached for Christ. There are nearly a quarter of a billion Sindhis worldwide.

Be still, and know that I am God; I will be exalted among the nations, I will be exalted in the earth. Psalm 46:10

* Sindh is home to many Punjabi Christians. Pray that they would reach out to the majority Sindi community around them.

* Pray that efforts to reach the Hindu Sindhis of India would result in thousands coming to Christ.

* Pray that the Prince of Peace would calm religious as well as ethnic tensions in the Sindh region.

* Pray that the Holy Spirit would soften the hearts of the Muslim Sindhis to the truth of the gospel.

* Pray that the Lord would raise up Christians from South Africa, Tanzania, Kenya, Uganda, the U.S., and Europe to reach out to the Sindhis in their midst.

Punjabi

Homeland: Punjab, India; Pakistan
Religion: Hinduism, Sikhism, Islam

In October 1995, Valson Abraham, President of India Gospel Outreach, held several days of evangelistic meetings in the Punjabi city of Lubhiana. He must have been amazed when thousands of Punjabi-speaking people responded to his call to follow Christ. Little did he know that on the same days he was holding these meetings, the AD 2000 movement had mobilised 30 million Christians to pray for the "Gateway Cities" of India as part of *Praying Through the Window II*. The day after these intercessors prayed for Amritsar, a city near Lubhiana, thousands of Hindus and Sikhs gave their hearts to Christ. A missionary working among the Sikh Punjabi reports, "We heard of many miraculous encounters of people receiving dreams and visions of the Lord, and healings and miracles in their lives."

Thank you, Father, for hearing the prayers of your saints. May your Kingdom be established among the Punjabi-speaking people today.

Nepali

Homeland: India, Nepal, Bhutan
Religion: Hinduism

Until recently, the isolated Himalayan nation of Nepal has resisted the gospel. In the mid-1700's, the government expelled all Nepali Christians. As late as 1940, there was only one Nepali Christian in the Hindu kingdom of Nepal. But then the dam broke. Since 1991, Nepalis and visitors have been free to profess and practice any religion, but not to proselytise. Today an estimated 100,000 people in Nepal worship the true and living God. Why the drastic change? One of the main reasons has been Christian medical work. In 1951 the king of Nepal allowed a medical team to enter the country. Since that time, Christian aid organisations have been providing much needed medical care in the name of Christ. The humble testimony of these Christian workers stood in stark contrast to the corruption of government officials. Hindu people groups have been touched with the gospel!

Jesus, thank you for using the medical work in Nepal to draw people to yourself. Please raise up a strong church for every Hindu and Buddhist people group in Nepal.

Newari

Homeland: Nepal
Religion: Hinduism, Buddhism, traditional religions

The half million Newari people of Nepal's Kathmandu Valley are known for their superior abilities trading on the international market. Most are well-educated, prosperous, and belong to the middle and higher Hindu castes. Many Newari people blend Buddhism, Hinduism, and indigenous beliefs in a fashion confusing to outsiders. They believe in ghosts, demons, evil spirits, witches, and a seemingly endless number of gods. An estimated 600 Newars are Christians. They only have access to portions of the Bible in their own language.

Lord, raise up workers who will complete the Newari Bible and produce more resources, like the Jesus film, to reach the Newari people.

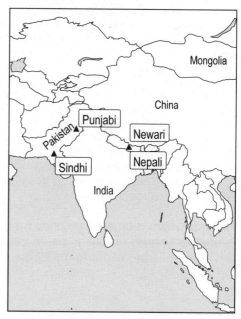

Hindko

Homeland: Pakistan, India
Religion: Islam

Photo Courtesy Bernice Condit.

Long shirt tails hang over baggy pants as Hindko-speaking men tend their plots or graze their animals on open land. With no fences, an adult or a child watches the grazing animals not only to see that they have good pasture but also to ensure that they do not destroy nearby crops. Since much of the area is mountainous, oxen and wooden ploughs are common on the small terraced fields. Even small tractors could not traverse these narrow paths. A guest might be offered tea with sugar and water-buffalo milk or perhaps even water-buffalo meat, although special occasions demand mutton.

Only a few of the roughly five million people who speak the Hindko language are well educated. The majority are illiterate. Most Hindko-speaking people live north of Pakistan's capital, Islamabad, but due to economic difficulties there, many of the men seek employment 900 miles away in the port city of Karachi. Because of this great distance, most men will return home to visit their families only once each year. In Karachi, many Hindko-speaking men find employment as taxi-drivers, while others are hired as watchmen to protect residences and businesses.

Most Hindko-speakers are Sunni Muslims. Nevertheless, many still seek practical results from variations of folk Islam. They revere holy men and their graves, hoping for answered prayers. Hindko-speakers might pray at traditional holy sites about infertility, a sick water buffalo, a son's school exams, or physical ailments.

A former nurse at Bach Christian Hospital became intrigued with the local language. She found a woman who could help her learn Hindko who had become a follower of Jesus some years before. This woman, along with several others, helped the nurse put the New Testament into Hindko. Gospel Recordings staff made several trips to the area and Hindko speakers sat many hours in make-shift studios to put the Hindko New Testament on cassettes.

May the nations be glad and sing for joy, for you rule the peoples justly and guide the nations of the earth. Psalm 67:4

• Pray for the Pakistan Bible Society as they print and distribute the Hindko New Testament. Ask the Lord of the Harvest to anoint it and use it mightily.

• Pray for the new effort to reach Hindko-speakers in Karachi. Away from home and family pressures, these men can be more open to the gospel. Pray also concerning ethnic tensions they face in Karachi.

• Pray that the Lord would raise up leaders among the few Hindko-speaking believers. Pray that they would find ways to attract other Hindko-speakers to the gospel.

• Ask God to bring both illiterate and educated Hindko-speaking families to himself.

Jats

Homeland: India, Pakistan
Religion: Hinduism, Islam, Sikhism

The Jats take their name from a Hindu caste of farmers. Although they share common origins and culture, the millions of Jat peoples living in south Asia are today separated by religious differences. Muslim Jat, who live primarily in Pakistan, follow the scriptures of the Koran, which they believe were revealed by Allah to the prophet Muhammad. In the Punjab area of India live Jats who follow Sikhism, a religion which draws on beliefs from both Islam and Hinduism. They practice tolerance of others, which can be seen at their places of worship where they offer free food and shelter. Those Jats who remain Hindu have a polytheistic, ceremonial religion. They believe that individuals cannot leave this earth for a better place without working their way up to the highest caste through reincarnation. In spite of the Jats' diversity of religious belief, only a small percent of the population is Christian.

Spirit of conviction, set a fire in the Jat people of India and Pakistan. Show them that their hope lies in Jesus Christ, and in him only.

Maithil

Homeland: India, Nepal
Religion: Hinduism, Islam

More than 20 million people speak the Maithili language. Primarily Hindu, these Maithili-speakers are among India's most devout Hindus and live rural, conservative lives. The landscape of northern Bihar, where 15 million Maithil live, is dotted by date and mango trees watered by Himalayan rivers. Many of its people are farmers, happy to share hospitality and the fruit of their land with visitors. Christian workers in northern Bihar have been preaching the gospel in the Hindi language for more than 80 years. However, only the educated Maithil can understand Hindi; poor, lower-caste Maithils have yet to hear the gospel in their own language. There are very few Maithil Christians.

Lord of the harvest, plant the seed of your gospel in the hearts of both low-caste and high-caste Maithil.

Tharu

Homeland: Nepal, India
Religion: Hinduism, Animism

Nearly three million Tharu people live on the edge of northwest India's forests and Nepal's southern plains. Tharus' lives are shaped by their connection to the environment. They farm the plains, trap animals in the forest, collect roots and herbs, and fish in small rivers and streams. Tharu women decorate the walls of their houses with colourful paintings of elephants, horses, parrots, and flowers. Married women have elaborate tattoos on their bodies. The majority of Tharus follow a mixture of Hinduism and Animism and focus on serving household gods and forest spirits, to whom they make offerings. There are many clans of Tharu. Such diversity makes evangelisation difficult.

Lord, we know the Tharu clans are not beyond the reach of your love and power. Redeem each of them for your glory!

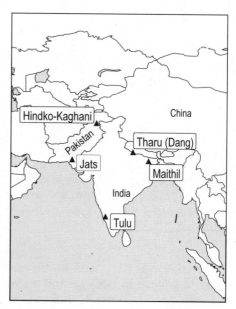

Urdu

Homeland: India, Pakistan
Religion: Islam

"Nine out of ten Muslims in India who make decisions to follow Jesus revert back to Islam," declared a Christian leader in north India. "The family and community pressure is too strong, and the church here doesn't know how to care for or meet the needs of these new converts leaving Islam."

Should this be surprising? For Urdu-speaking Muslim communities, life revolves around the family—from a child's first days when the local *imam* (Muslim leader) prays over him in the family home, to his death and a funeral full of wailing and mourning, the members of his extended family live out life together, often sharing a compound with many relatives. Independent actions and decisions are rare, and marriages are arranged by one's parents. Many work in family businesses, passed down for generations.

While still a small minority in this vast country, more Muslims live in India than in the whole Middle East. Muslims dominate both Pakistan and Bangladesh, where it is illegal for them to convert to Christianity. While conversion is legal in India, Muslims interested in Christianity in all three countries face severe family and community pressure. Making an independent decision for Christ is social suicide. Converts lose family, jobs, and reputations, and may be physically abused.

Normal life becomes almost impossible. How can a single convert to Christianity get married if his family will not even speak to him, much less arrange his marriage? How can a new convert find a job when everyone in his community knows he is the one who disgraced his family by leaving their religion for another? How will his children be educated when none of the schools in his neighbourhood will admit infidels? Where will he be buried, when all of the nearby cemeteries are for Muslims only?

The dominance of the family in Urdu-speaking Muslim communities is by no means unique, and need not be a barrier to the gospel. During the time of Jesus decisions were made together by the family and community, rarely by a single individual.

**The jailer was filled with joy because he had come to believe in God—he and his whole family.
Acts 16:34b**

* Ask God to move whole communities to repent and confess Jesus as Lord together.

* Pray that Muslims would encounter Christ and lead their families to him.

* Pray that the Lord would raise up many churches to adopt India's Muslim peoples.

* Pray that God would one day send out Christian missionaries from the Urdu-speaking communities of North India to other Muslims around the globe.

* Indians consider children their most valuable commodity. Pray for Christian ministries to reach Indian Muslims by caring for their children's needs.

Muslims of Deccan

Homeland: South India
Religion: Islam

Muslims of India's arid Deccan Plateau are among the poorest of the poor. Yet this was not always so. For 600 years a Decanni Muslim dynasty ruled the princely state of Hyderabad, and, as a minority people, they dominated government, military, and business circles until 1948. Decanni Muslims lost much of their political power when other Muslims fled to Pakistan and what is now Bangladesh, and Hindus dominated India. Today most Deccani work in low-status jobs such as blacksmiths or shopkeepers. Most of the Christians in India live in the south, but little is being done to reach their Muslim neighbours.

Holy Spirit, move the hearts of many Indian believers to penetrate the tightly knit Deccan Muslim communities.

Kashmiri

Homeland: India, Pakistan
Religion: Islam, Hinduism

Amid the western Himalayas, the valley of Kashmir is a smooth, oval emerald set in a forest of towering peaks. Called the paradise of the Indies with pine forests, deep lakes, flower carpeted meadows, and fields of iridescent saffron, Indians today long to visit there and it serves as the setting for countless romantic films. Before the 8th century this site became a centre of Brahmin learning and later a Muslim cultural centre as well. Muslims, Hindus, Sikhs, and others have all influenced Kashmiri cultural development. In 1947, when Britain divided the Indian subcontinent into India and Pakistan, a dispute over Kashmir resulted in millions of deaths in bloody riots. Today Kashmiri Muslims fight for an independent Kashmir, and many are willing to die for the cause. This has led to atrocities committed by both the Kashmiri and the Indian government, resulting in terrorism, refugee camps, and severe economic hardships.

Lord, as the Prince of Peace, bring the Kashmiri into the land that is their true inheri-
tance and use these current hardships to lead Kashmiri to yourself.

Maldivian

Homeland: Maldive Islands
Religion: Islam

The Maldivian people give their name to the Maldive islands, some 2,000 islands south west of the tip of India. Of all the islands, only 202 are habitable and the highest point is only six feet above sea level. Islam came to the Maldives through 12th century Arab traders and now dominates the nation. The government enforces allegiance to Islam and restricts Christian media and literature even among the expatriate community. Maldives remains one of the most restricted Muslim countries in the world. Most Maldivians earn their living through fishing, shipping, and tourism. Many keep animistic practices, trusting charms, mantras, and *fandita* or spirit men, to protect them from evil spirits. Some 85 percent of their marriages end in divorce, a rate among the highest in the world.

God of glory, among the Maldivians there is no sweet aroma of praise to you. Touch their hearts to give you the praise you are due.

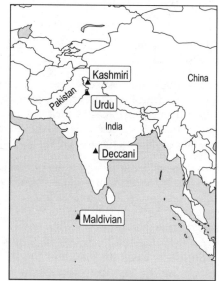

Chamar

Homeland: India
Religion: Hinduism

Ravi's family is supported by the sale of beautifully worked leather products, which they carefully make by hand. In spite of their artistry, the family is little respected in their community. Ravi is a Chamar, a member of the "untouchable" caste of leather-workers. People of higher caste consider the millions of Chamar, scattered throughout India, unclean. The Chamar are despised because of their work skinning and tanning animal hides, which involves handling the carcasses of animals.

Hindus believe that those who handle unclean objects, such as the leather Ravi's family handles, are defiled. No Indian would chose such a trade; the Chamar are born to it. Hindu teachings explain that the Chamar were born into their families as punishment for the evil deeds of their past lives. They therefore deserve to be treated poorly.

The Chamar and other *Dalits*, or oppressed people, as they call themselves, often live on the outskirts of towns and villages. Some Dalits, like Ravi, are leather-workers, while others are responsible for burying or cremating the dead, or scavenge for a living. When Dalits have their own villages, these communities are enclosed by a high wall to protect other castes from being polluted by the sight of them. In some cases, Dalits have been forbidden to use public roads or to leave their homes without ringing a bell to signal their approach. In 1949 the Indian government passed laws forbidding the use of the term "untouchables" and prohibiting discrimination against the Dalit. Caste barriers have now relaxed to the point where Dalit children may attend local schools.

Enough of these untouchables came to Christ through people movements in the last century to brand Christianity as the religion of despised classes in the eyes of many Indians. Yet today many Dalit groups remain totally unreached with the gospel.

While the poverty and rejection of the Chamar and other Dalits embitters some, it leaves others hungry for the acceptance and inheritance Jesus offers. May many Chamar hear and rejoice in the knowledge that Jesus can make them clean!

So the last will be first, and the first will be last. Matthew 20:16

• We rejoice that the Chamar people will one day know justice. Pray against bitterness and for their protection from abuse from higher castes within their communities.

• Thank God for the protection of the Indian government. Pray that more Dalits would learn how to read and acquire skills to improve their lives and provide for their families.

• Pray for the spread of the gospel among Dalit. Thank God for the many Dalit whom he has drawn to himself in the past, and ask him to equip them to reach others.

• Pray for peace and respect among the multitude of castes and tribes in the vast nation of India.

Balmiki

Homeland: India
Religion: Hindusim

Radia was born into a world that always works. At age ten, she has already worked for five years as a sweeper. Her employer belongs to a higher middle class caste. There she does the washing, cleaning, sweeping, and shopping. She earns only 21 rupees per month, which she hands over to her mother for food and clothing. Radia does not play any childhood games. She has no toys, no money, no education, and no entertainment. Radia is a member of the Balmiki caste, a sweeper or sanitation worker. Like the leather-workers, sweepers are outcasts, considered unclean by other Hindus. Most sweepers, like Radia, live in the present moment, unaware that there are luxuries in life. Their lives revolve around work, the next meal, and a dry place to lay their head in the monsoons. They live in poverty and without education. The Balmiki have little or no knowledge of the Bible or Jesus. Thankfully, a number of Christian agencies are rising to the challenge of reaching these people, trying to reach entire families for Jesus.

God of hope, show the Balmiki the powerful truth of your love for them.

Landless Labourers

Homeland: India
Religion: Hinduism

While many of India's Hindus define themselves and others by caste or language, both of these are often linked to occupation. Many Indians live in communities with others who make their living in the same way. When the gospel comes into an Indian society, it often spreads through these occupational communities. Even in their loss of an occupation, groups like the landless labourers see themselves as having something in common and feel camaraderie with one another. These landless labourers find their place in Indian society as the result of an extremely powerful landlord class established by the British. Today this class has thwarted the government attempts at land reform. Theoretically, feudalism has been abolished and replaced with fair limits on the amount of land an individual can own. In reality the landlord class continues to monopolise the agricultural market. The traditional *jajmni* system, through which landless labourers bartered their services for food and clothing, has disappeared. Poor farmers cannot afford expensive seed and fertiliser, machines, and irrigation systems. They are forced to either work for the more successful farmers or seek another role in society. Each year more migrants move to the large cities of Bombay, Calcutta, and Delhi looking for work.

Lord, you are the refuge for the oppressed. Provide employment and salvation for these workers.

Brahmin

Photo Courtesy John Fries, Procla-Media / YWAM.

Homeland: India
Religion: Hinduism

My name is Anjum. I am a Brahmin. I was born to parents renowned in our community for their ardent pursuit of Hinduism. I also blindly joined them in worshipping the idols for 18 years. Then while studying a computer course, I met a Christian student named Dilip. He told me about his faith in a living God, not an idol. Although I hated Christianity, I politely attended church with him on occasion.

We parted ways after graduation, but to our surprise we were hired by the same software firm a year later. Soon we began to share a room, and Dilip shared with me about God from the Bible and from his life. He took me to a meeting where I felt the presence of God and saw people healed before my eyes. I became a follower of Jesus. When I shared my faith with my family, they were livid and seemingly endless problems began. But I have kept praying for them. Now my mother has accepted Christ and my brother, quite a strong Hindu, is showing interest in the Bible!

As for me, my life is new, with a purpose to glorify God in all things. I have trusted my future, my marriage to a believer, and my destiny into the hands of him who is the author and perfecter of my faith.

Brahmins from families like Anjum's reign at the top of the four-tiered Hindu caste system that still influences nearly every aspect of Indian life. Their status carries advantage and responsibility that few outside of a Hindu background can imagine. They are considered ritualistically pure, an asset for a priestly class. They are also known to be wise, able to read and interpret the scriptures. Today Brahmins fill many different roles in Indian society, often exercising great power and influence.

Perhaps it is in part because of their privileged status that few Brahmins have followed Jesus. To a Brahmin considering the claims of Christ, the price must seem great. Although their lives seem glorious, Brahmins who read the scripture must see the truth of Romans 3:23, that "all have sinned and fall short of the glory of God." May these priests of India come to know and celebrate the next verse as well, finding themselves "justified freely by his grace through the redemption that came by Jesus Christ."

Where, then, is boasting? It is excluded. On what principle? On that of observing the law? No, but on that of faith. For we maintain that a man is justified by faith apart from observing the law.
Romans 3:27-28

• Ask God to thrust forth labourers, both Indians and foreigners, into his harvest field among the Brahmins.

• Pray that more and more Brahmins would be compelled by a sense of their sin and the contrasting glory of God to put aside their idols and give their lives whole-heartedly to him.

• Pray for enduring and maturing faith for Brahmin believers such as Anjum. Ask God to redeem and even broaden their influence for Jesus.

• Pray that the Spirit of God would do what only he can do to bring a biblical sense of brotherhood and a godly unity of purpose to the disparate believers from low and high castes.

Middle Classes

Homeland: India
Religion: Hinduism

Like college graduates around the world Anil faced his new life with mixed emotion. On the one hand, he now possessed freedom like never before; but with this freedom came responsibility. Anil was expected to take over his father's business. Once wealthy, Anil's grandfather had been stripped of land and titles not long after Indian independence in 1947. Now, walking home from his last class and a visit to the temple, Anil imagined what life must have been like for his grandfather. Managing his father's firm was a long way from the ruling and rampaging of his ancestors. Yet Anil is part of India's rapidly growing consumer class and his conquests may include such luxuries as a comfortable apartment, a nice private car, and household appliances.

Lord, work in the hearts of these business-men to, like Paul, consider all things a loss compared to the surpassing greatness of knowing Christ.

Business Communities

Homeland: India
Religion: Hinduism, Islam

"You can trust the devil, but you can't trust a Bohra!" say Indians with a laugh, revealing the reputation of this Muslim people and

their place in the business communities of India. Bohras, who live in the major cities of western India, are famous for their shrewd-ness in business and for their allegiance to their spiritual leader, the Syedna. The Bohras belong to their own Muslim sect. All aspects of a faithful Bohra's life fall under the author-ity of the Syedna, including his family's business, his marriage, and his children's names. The Syedna has little grace for behav-iour outside the community norm. If someone began to follow Jesus, he would have to be very careful to avoid excommuni-cation. But if a new convert is removed from the community, he no longer has the oppor-tunity to influence his extended family and business associates.

Spirit, open hearts among India's growing and dynamic business communities, espe-cially calling Bohras into relationship with you. Help them know how to walk with you while staying in relationship with their com-munity.

Urban Communities

Homeland: India
Religion: Hinduism, Islam

One of India's fastest growing segments are urban communities. In this fast paced and changing environment caste lines become more blurred. Nevertheless, among the core of India's city-dwelling communities are a people called the Marwaris. In communities radiating from their homeland in the state of Rajhastan, Marwaris have moved into posi-tions of economic influence in most Indian cities. Although they are a relatively small and close-knit group of people, the frugality and financial expertise shown by the Mar-waris has vaulted them into the upper echelons of Indian society and power. In-creasingly India turns to the Marwari for financial direction. Some of the richest men in India are Marwaris, but few have begun to follow the Lord.

Father, Jesus said that with man it might be impossible, but with you, all things are pos-sible. Please bring many Marwaris into your kingdom.

Photo Courtesy John Fries, Procla-Media / YWAM.

Pashtun

Homeland: Afghanistan, Pakistan
Religion: Sunni Islam

The sweet green tea was just settling in Omar's throat when he heard the noise. The clatter from the manual water pump stopped abruptly. Two men were fighting. Omar set down his fresh *nan* bread and waited to see what would happen.

His sense of relaxed calm evaporated completely with the shot of a gun. One man was dead and the other wrestled to the ground and restrained by bystanders who sent a message to the nearby police station. The sun grew hot, but the dry air hid the heat.

The dead man's mother arrived to grieve, wailing loudly with the pain of her sorrow. An army rifle was placed in her shaking hands; soon, another shot tore the once calm day. She had avenged her son's death by killing his enemy, and family honour was restored. Two men were buried that evening. Allah was pleased, however, because he will not forgive those who do not protect their family's honour. Or will he?

Many Pashtun families in Afghanistan value family honour above all else. Family pride is behind the hospitality lavished on visitors. It is also behind the practice of keeping all adult women covered decently.

Millions of Pashto-speaking families, also known as Pashtun, Pathan, or Afghan, live in the countries of Afghanistan, Pakistan, The United Arab Emirates, Iran, and Tajikistan, in hundreds of clans. While the *Jesus* film is available in Western Pashto, it has not been widely distributed. At least a portion of the Bible has been translated into the dialects of most Pashto-speaking people groups, but finding a Bible in Afghanistan is not easy. There are very few Pashtun believers, and nearly all of these live outside of Afghanistan. As of 1996, there were only a dozen Christian missionaries in Afghanistan who could speak the Pashto language.

My salvation and my honor depend on God; he is my mighty rock, my refuge. Psalm 62:7

- Pray for the breaking of the cycle of blood revenge in this war torn land.

- Pray that heads of households would understand the forgiveness found in Jesus' blood, and that women and children interested in Jesus would not suffer for it.

- There is a small Pashto-speaking church in Pakistan. Pray for growth and unity for this small fellowship and its leaders.

- Pray for the Nuristani and Pashai peoples who have never had a church or missions work.

- Pray for these fierce fighters to enter into the spiritual battle on the side of the kingdom of God.

Baluch

Homeland: Pakistan
Religion: Sunni Islam

Each year millions of Baluch celebrate *Eid ul Azha* or the Sacrifice Holiday. On this day Muslim families around the world kill a sheep or goat, much as Abraham sacrificed the ram God provided. Each family divides the meat from the butchered animal into three portions: one for the needy, one for their neighbours, and one for the family. The next few days are filled with feasting on meats prepared in tasty traditional dishes. Many Baluch follow this custom even though they do not really understand the reasons behind it. "It's tradition," they explain.

Father, reveal to the Baluch your sacrifice that ended sacrifices. Bless those who are reaching out to the Baluch and anoint the radio programs which go where there are no missionaries.

Brahui

Homeland: Pakistan, Afghanistan
Religion: Islam

A century ago all Brahuis, or Kur Galli, were nomads and herders. Today many Brahui live in settled villages. Physically, Brahui tribesmen resemble their Baluch and Pashtun neighbours. They speak their own language, related to the Dravidian languages of distant south India. One mission is working among the Brahui people, but at present only a handful of the Brahui are Christian.

Spirit, mould these few Brahui believers into a strong and multiplying church. Give them boldness and wisdom to share rightly to others within their culture.

Aimaq

Homeland: Afghanistan, Iran
Religion: Sunni Islam

The Aimaq people, also known as Jamshidi or Teymur, are semi-nomadic herders from a variety of smaller tribes and clans, totalling more than a million people. They herd sheep, goats, and horses. They also weave elegant and unique carpets by hand. Living in *yurts*, tents made of animal hair, they usually move their herds to the mountains in the summer and back down to the valley in the fall. There are no known believers or churches and no known Christian work focusing on them.

Lord, forgive us for neglecting peoples like the Aimaq. Raise up workers to live among them, learn their languages, and live out your love like human love letters.

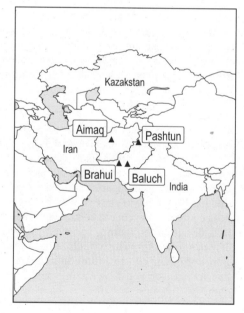

Photo Courtesy Bernice Condit.

Persian

Homeland: Iran
Religion: Islam

"You're crazy for calling yourself a Christian, Salima. Don't you know you could be killed for that?"

"Ibrahim," Salima calmly replied to her younger brother, "I'm 63 years old, and I've finally found the truth. If they must, let them kill me."

Ibrahim turned and pleaded to Salima's husband, Reza, a retired colonel, "Uncle, can't you see what your wife is doing?"

"Ah, I think she's found the right road," Reza responded. "And I'm thinking about going that way, too."

Salima is among an increasing number of Iranians who are discovering the striking love of Jesus. Since the Islamic revolution in 1979, many Iranians have become open to the life that the Lord offers. In spite of this increasing interest in the gospel, only a very small percent of the 25 million Persian Iranis are believers. An even lower percentage of believers is found among minority ethnic groups who make up nearly half of Iran's population. Yet their growing interest in Jesus has not gone unnoticed. Pressure on the church has intensified, causing many to flee for their lives, while others have forfeited their lives on earth for the gospel.

To outside eyes it may appear that the political subjugation of the ancient nation of Persia to Islam is a victory for Satan, but God has other plans. Remember the story of Esther, the young Jew who became queen of Persia when Haman was plotting to annihilate her people? The same God has his people in place to win the day for his name: he is equipping the church in Iran, Persian believers who have fled to other nations, and even you and me as we play our part by praying for such a day as this. Take the words of Esther's uncle, Mordecai to heart: "Perhaps for this very reason you have been brought into the kingdom."

Then the church ... enjoyed a time of peace. It was strengthened; and encouraged by the Holy Spirit, it grew in numbers, living in the fear of the Lord. Acts 9:31

• Pray for the valiant church which has seen pastors killed and many believers fleeing the country. Pray also for revival in the Orthodox and Armenian churches.

• Of the 65,000 villages in Iran, maybe six have a Christian presence. Pray for effective radio and television broadcasts as well as sensitive and appropriate evangelistic efforts by believers from Iran and elsewhere.

• Pray for the thousands who have fled the Iranian regime. Many are remarkably open to the gospel; new fellowships have come to life around the world!

• God put great honour and glory into the ancient culture of Persia. Pray that he would be again glorified through it.

Tajik

Homeland: Tajikistan, Uzbekistan, Afghanistan, Iran
Religion: Islam, Animism

"I had a dream last night," announced the raspy voice on the line. The caller's accent identified him as a Tajik seeker who had attended Amir's Bible study the night before. "A white-robed man approached me, book in hand. When I asked who he was, he replied, 'Jesus.' He extended his hand toward me and said, 'Write your name in the book.' Can you tell me the meaning of this dream?" Amir smiled and began to tell his Tajik friend about the Book of Life into which believers names are written. When the man came to the study two days later, he requested a Bible, declaring, "I want to become a follower of Jesus."

Father, glorify yourself by revealing Jesus to the Tajik people through the Bible and through dreams and visions. Raise up many Tajiks who can lead Bible studies.

Mazanderani

Homeland: Iran
Religion: Islam

The 3.2 million Mazanderani people live primarily in the northern reaches of Iran just south of the Caspian Sea. Those who are educated speak Farsi, the national language, but many, especially women, speak only their native Mazanderani language. They are intensely devoted to their families and to the strict tenets of Shi'a Islam. The Mazanderani live and die virtually untouched by the gospel. Some have access to Christian radio broadcasts, but only in Farsi. There are no broadcasts in Mazanderani and no known missionaries focusing on this huge unreached people group. Paul's words in Romans 10:12-14 ring sombre and true for the Mazaderani: "the same Lord is Lord of all and richly blesses all who call on him, for, 'Everyone who calls on the name of the Lord will be saved.' ... And how can they believe in the one of whom they have not heard?"

Lord of the Harvest, we ask that you would thrust forth labourers into the harvest field of the Mazanderani.

Hazara

Homeland: Afghanistan, Iran
Religion: Islam

As he topped the small rise, Mohamad's village came into view. It was evening, and the sun, as well as his long winter of work in the city, was behind him. For the next several months he would live with his family and the flocks, searching out green pasture for the sheep and clean air to ease the distress of his tuberculosis. Mohamad is one of 1.8 million Hazara people living in Afghanistan. They are descendants of Ghengis Khan and nearly all are Muslim. By some reports the Hazara people are more responsive than many Muslims to the gospel. Recent efforts have been made by Christians to minister to their medical needs and a limited amount of Christian radio now reaches them. Some Hazara are also being reached in countries like Pakistan, India, and the United States.

Christ, please lead these shepherds by the still waters and the green pastures of which David sang in Psalm 23.

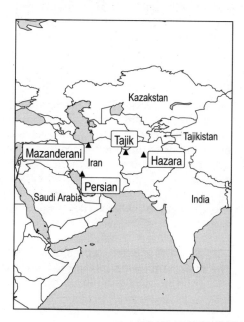

Kurds

Homeland: Kurdistan (Turkey, Iran, Iraq, Syria)
Religion: Sunni Muslim

Photo Courtesy Patty Fraats, People International.

The great Kurdish hero, *Saladdin*, is famous throughout the Muslim world for his victory over the Crusaders and for liberating Jerusalem. He is also known for his chivalry and generosity. For most of their history, however, the Kurds have known little victory, and have instead been pawns trapped between the Persian (Iranian) and Ottoman (Turkish) empires.

Mountainous Kurdistan is a natural cross-roads: the source of two great rivers mentioned in the Bible, the Tigris and Euphrates, and the location of Mount Ararat. Here roads and passes connect the Mediterranean with the Caucasus. It is a beautiful land of high mountains, plateaux and valleys, rivers and lakes. The climate is beautiful but harsh—cold and snowy in the winter, hot in the summer.

There is only one problem: Kurdistan is not a country, and the political forces which control it will not release it. Though the Kurds number in the tens of millions, they are minorities in each of the countries in which they live. As a result, they have been persecuted for hundreds of years, experiencing everything from broken promises and forced relocation to outright genocide.

An old Kurdish proverb says, "The Kurds have no friends except the mountains." Yet today a number of churches and agencies from around the world have begun to focus on the needs of the Kurds, organising assistance on a number of levels. Any one of these groups alone could accomplish very little for the Kurds, but because they have resolved to work together across denominational and international borders, they are beginning to see success.

In his hand are the depths of the earth, and the mountain peaks belong to him. Psalm 95:4

- Pray for opportunity, unity, and fruit for the partnership of churches and agencies working with Kurds.

- Pray for the national and local leaders where Kurds live, that they would show grace, compassion, and mercy rather than oppression and racism.

- Pray for the Kurdish language radio broadcasts, that many would listen, and that those who respond could have opportunity to learn more.

- Only one of the many Kurdish dialects has the *Jesus* Film translated. Because most Kurds are illiterate, pray especially for this powerful tool to be made available, as well as cassette tapes in local dialects.

- Though some dialects have Bible portions translated, none have a complete Bible. Pray especially for *Dimli*-speaking Kurds in Turkey, and their Bible translation which is in progress.

Luri

Homeland: Iran
Religion: Islam

Among the nearly five million Luri people of Iran, there are no known Christians. Radio broadcasts and the witnessing efforts of Luri believers from neighbouring Iraq have touched only one in every ten, leaving 90 percent with no knowledge of the gospel. Once nomads known for great ferocity, today most Luris are Shiite Muslims and have settled in the cities and villages of south estern Iran. Recent efforts of some mission agencies have increased awareness of the Luris and may result in missionaries at last being sent out to them.

Father, you created the Luris. Please bring them into your kingdom, that they might know abundant life and lift abundant praise to your name.

Gilaki

Homeland: Iran
Religion: Shi'a Islam

The hot sun beat down on the Gilaki fisherman and shimmered in his eyes off the Caspian Sea. He thought of his son who had just moved to Rasht to work in the silk factory. Why would he leave the beauty of the Caspian for the noise of the city? The fisherman glanced back toward the green and forested coast and knew he could never be happy in a city. The Gilaki, numbering around three million, live in north western Iran. Besides fishing, they farm crops and keep a few animals. Educated Gilaki men can read Farsi, but the Gilaki language is not yet in written form. Nevertheless, a Bible translation may be in progress and some Christian programs have been recorded on cassettes. Sponsors are being sought for a much-needed radio ministry, perhaps the most strategic way to reach many Gilaki. Remember also those who speak the Gilashi dialect living nearby in the mountains.

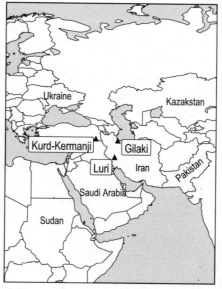

Holy Spirit, call these fishermen into Christ's kingdom, teaching them to fish for men! Raise up the finances and people to sustain a Christian radio program in Gilaki.

Unknown

Homeland: All Across the 10/40 Window
Religion: Islam, Hindu, Buddhist, Animist

Researchers have catalogued thousands of ethnic groups in the world, and this process has been greatly assisted by computer technology. However, it is quite possible that there are hundreds if not thousands of groups which we still know nothing about. Many of these groups are small but others are simply hidden. While some information is becoming available for other groups, it is simply not enough to help mission strategists, mobilisers, and church planters plan effectively. Even what we think we know we sometimes later find to have been false. Many of these hidden or unknown groups are the ones who most need the gospel. Even though God has been working for centuries in their culture preparing for his arrival, the church is still completely unaware of their presence.

Sovereign God, we lift up to you the hundreds of peoples, entire tribes, about which we do not know. Continue to work in their midst preparing them for the arrival of the gospel, and working in our midst to not fall back from the task you gave us.

Photo Courtesy Jack Hollingsworth for OMF International.

Uygur

Homeland: Northwest China, Kazakstan, Central Asia
Religion: Islam, Animism

In the deserts and mountains of northwest China live the third-largest of China's ethnic minority nationalities, the more than seven million Uygurs. Uygurs descend from Silk Road merchants who traded Central Asian horses for Chinese silk and jade. Uygur traders still dominate the bazaars of Xinjiang Province, where the air is heavy with the smell of hot tea, mutton kebabs, and a flat bread called *nan*. The majority, however, cultivate cotton, grapes, melons, and other fruit through an ingenious system of irrigation that pipes water from the mountains into the desert oases.

The Uygurs are related in race, culture, and language to the Turkic peoples of Central Asia. Like most Central Asians, the Uygurs practice folk Islam, a blend of Muslim beliefs and animistic rituals. The men wear an embroidered cap called a *doppa* while the most traditional of the women cover their faces with a veil.

Xinjiang province, the Uygur homeland, is rich in minerals and is a strategic defence zone for China's military. Since coming under Chinese control in the 1880's, the Uygurs and other minority groups have periodically suffered persecution. Chinese national policy tolerates the cultures and languages of minority groups, but a strong current of mutual resentment remains between the Uygurs and the Chinese majority. In recent years the government has brought millions of ethnic Chinese into Xianjiang, diluting Uygur influence.

Although government restrictions and Islamic renewal hamper efforts to reach the Uygurs in China, media and translation projects hold promise. Uygurs in Kazakstan show signs of great spiritual hunger and are responding to the gospel. Many have been baptised and entire families converted.

Know that the LORD is God. It is he who made us, and we are his; we are his people, the sheep of his pasture. Psalm 100:3

- Pray that more Uygurs in Central Asia and Kazakstan would follow Christ and become missionaries to Uygurs in China.

- Pray for reconciliation between Uygurs and Chinese, and that Chinese Christians might minister to Uygurs.

- Uygurs are often shielded from foreign visitors who are looked on suspiciously by the government. Pray for creative access strategies to bring more labourers to this harvest field.

- Pray for the few Uygur believers to persevere in their faith despite great pressure from their families and Muslim communities.

- Pray that community leaders would embrace Christ as Saviour and Lord, leading a cultural movement to faith in Christ.

Kazak

Homeland: Kazakstan, Northwest China
Religion: Islam, Animism

As tent-dwelling nomads, the Kazaks followed their herds across the Central Asian steppes from summer mountain pastures to winter valleys. When conquered by Russian Tsars and eventually incorporated into the Soviet Union, they gradually settled into towns, cities, and agricultural communities, but not without struggle. Soviet "collectivisation" brought mass starvation and ecological disasters. Nuclear test sites and space launch facilities built in Kazakstan contaminated many towns with radioactive poison. Today the Kazaks are trying to forge a new identity. They have invited Western businesses to invest in new private industries, but habits of bureaucracy and inefficiency make growth slow. The secular government allows religious freedom; many Kazak congregations have grown throughout the country. Kazak Bibles and other literature are needed to meet the growing spiritual hunger.

Christ, please keep this window of opportunity open and plant a vibrant church in every Kazak village and town.

Kyrgyz

Homeland: Kyrgyzstan
Religion: Islam,
    Animism

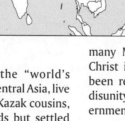

Settled in the valleys of the "world's rooftop," the high ranges of Central Asia, live the Kyrgyz people. Like their Kazak cousins, the Kyrgyz were once nomads but settled during Russian rule. Few Kyrgyz live in cities. Even the capital of Kyrgyzstan, Bishkek, is home to more Russians and Ukranians than Kyrgyz, a cause of ethnic tension since the republic's independence from Soviet rule in 1991. Moving from communism to democracy has been painful. Although the country is rich in minerals including gold and coal, it lacks the means to bring this wealth to world markets. The resulting poverty has encouraged some citizens to turn to drug trafficking. Even though the Kyrgyz are traditionally Muslim, the secular government currently allows freedom of religion, but restrictions are tightening. Few of the dozen or so churches in Kyrgyzstan are reaching ethnic Kyrgyz or working outside of the capital, Bishkek.

Spirit, train national leaders, and give them a vision to reach the many rural Kyrgyz.

Mongolian

Homeland: Mongolia, China
Religion: Tibetan Buddhism

Seven centuries ago the Mongol hordes of Ghenghis Khan overran Asia from the Danube River to the Pacific Ocean. Mongol culture dominated China, India, Central Asia, and the Middle East. For many years, however, Mongolians lived in relative obscurity in the shadow of Russia and China. Fewer than two million Mongolians live in Outer Mongolia, while more than five million live in Inner Mongolia, a province of China. Perhaps half of Mongolians are nomadic, living in felt tents they call *gers* and depending on the strength of their horses, in which they take great pride. Since its independence from Soviet domination, Outer Mongolia has returned to its traditional religion, Tibetan Buddhism. Although many Mongolians have come to faith in Christ in recent years, church growth has been restricted by a revival of Buddhism, disunity among Christian workers, and government opposition.

Jesus, let your body in Mongolia experience the unity you prayed for in John 17 and grant them the freedom they need to worship you.

Uzbek

Homeland: Uzbekistan, Afghanistan,
   Tajikistan
Religion: Islam, Animism

"Alisheer, quickly! Bring the sheep! Uncle Babur and I are ready to slaughter it." Father wanted me to help! Heart beating, I raced through the courtyard past the latrine to the animal pen. A ram bleated at me as I tripped over the feed bucket and crashed into the gate. "Poor sheep," I told him, "you bleat at me now, but in the afterlife you will help us cross into paradise. Remember how well you were treated under our care." I reached for a rope hanging beside the gate and threw it round his neck, then dragged the animal back to Father and Uncle Babur. We were about to take another step closer to paradise...

Alisheer and his family are Uzbeks, the most numerous of all the Central Asian Turkic peoples. Modern Uzbeks descend from the marriage of Mongol warriors and farmers with Persian city dwellers centuries ago. The Uzbeks have a rich language and culture, but learned to speak Russian during the years of Russian and Soviet rule. Only now is Uzbek replacing Russian as the language of education and government. While 80 percent of the citizens of Uzbekistan are Uzbeks, they share their nation with Tajiks, Russians, and other nationalities.

The Uzbeks are proud to be Muslim, but seek spiritual power from traditions far older than Islam. Uzbek children wear special bracelets to protect themselves from the evil eye and the influence of *jinn* (demons). The graves of saints are considered especially powerful and are visited by students hoping for good luck on their exams, barren women hoping to conceive, and fathers praying for their sick children. More than 60 years of Marxism have left their mark on Uzbek spirituality, however. Some Uzbeks say, "I'm a Muslim, but I don't believe in God."

**In that day they will say, "Surely this is our God; we trusted in him, and he saved us. This is the LORD, we trusted in him; let us rejoice and be glad in his salvation."
Isaiah 25:9**

• Pray that the millions of Uzbeks who have never heard the gospel might soon hear and believe in the one true God.

• Pray for unity among the churches of Uzbekistan, and ask God to raise up more wise and godly leaders who would shepherd their flocks well, preparing the next generation for ministry.

• New indigenous fellowships of former Muslims have begun in the last five years, in contrast to established Russian churches. Pray that their leaders would continue to grow in the grace and knowledge of Christ.

• Two-thirds of all Uzbeks live in villages of 2500 or less, concentrated in the Ferghana valley. Pray for thriving, indigenous churches among these village Uzbeks.

Tatar-Related Peoples

Homeland: Russia, Uzbekistan, Kazakstan, Ukraine

Religio n: Islam, Secularism

"THWUUUNG—the door of the box car slammed shut, the sound muffled by the bodies pressed all round me. My eyes strained in the blackness. The air in the box car was stale and heavy. I couldn't see my hand in front of my face, even if I could have moved my arm to get it there. My father was dead; my mother and brothers, all murdered in front of me by the soldiers. Uzbekistan, where they were sending me, seemed a lifetime away. My crime? I was Tatar."

Eager to create a new Soviet man, loyal only to the Union, Soviet leaders used genocide and mass deportation to neutralise nationalities they perceived as a threat. Many Tatars—a name Russians gave to all the Turkic Muslims living west of the Ural mountains—were victims of this strategy. Stalin accused the Crimean Tatars of conspiring with Hitler in World War II, and had them deported to Central Asia. Perhaps because of this separation from their homeland, Crimean Tatars have been more Russified than other Muslim peoples. Some are indistinguishable from their Russian neighbours.

Today more than eight million Tatars and related people live in the Russian republic. The Kazan Tatars and the Bashkirs live along the Volga river, and have autonomous republics within the Russian Federation. Siberian Tatars are descended from Mongol warriors who conquered Siberia in the 13th century.

Kazan Tatars

Since Ivan the Terrible destroyed the Kazan Khanate in 1552, Kazan Tatars have harboured great animosity towards Russians. Now,

an Islamic renaissance among them provides a means to maintain a distinct identity. Because Kazan Tatars view Christianity as a Russian religion, the few who convert and join the Russian Orthodox Church are considered cultural traitors. The Gospel of John has recently been translated into Tatar and is already in short supply. Other books of the Bible will be available soon.

Lord, thank you for the good response to the Gospel of John. Put a thirst for truth in the hearts of many Kazan Tatars.

Bashkir

The Bashkir were considered lower-class Tatars until the 1920's, when the Soviet Union declared them a separate people. After being looked down on for so long by Kazan Tatars, the Bashkir are proud of their separate status. The Bashkir capital, Ufa, is a centre of Islam in Russia.

Jesus, you are lord of the Bashkir. Move among them in grace and mercy.

Crimean Tatars

Many Tatars are returning to Crimea, where they are resented by Ukranians living there. Those remaining in Central Asia feel threatened by the nationalism of their Kazak and Uzbek hosts.

The Crimean Tatars are helpless and harassed, like sheep without a shepherd. Good Shepherd, we pray for their healing and redemption.

Siberian Tatars

The Siberian Tatars exhibit less animosity towards Russians than other Tatars do, and are consequently more open, on the whole, to Christianity.

Lord of the harvest, increase the openness and spiritual hunger of Siberian Tatars, and lead the Russian church to rightly reach out to them.

Turks

Homeland: Turkey
Religion: Islam

Aysegul studies engineering in a Turkish city. She hopes to find a good job after graduating so that she can have a comfortable life and support her parents as they grow older. Aysegul's parents live in the small town where she grew up on the Mediterranean coast.

This summer she brought an American friend to visit her hometown. Cindy soon learned that she was their first foreign visitor ever. Children flocked around the girls. Aysegul introduced Cindy to many people, most of them her own relatives. Cindy wondered if anyone there had ever heard the good news of Jesus. She prayed for an opportunity to share Christ with her Turkish friend.

Although Turkey is officially a secular state, more than 99 percent of its citizens are Muslim, totaling about 60 million. In spite of an official policy of religious freedom, believers suffer persecution and sometimes imprisonment for their faith.

Geographically, Turkey is in a strategic position, straddling the European and Asian continents and bordered by four seas. Turks are proud of their history, remembering the strength of the powerful general Kemal Ataturk, who established the democratic republic at the end of World War I. Ataturk brought the Turks a strong ethnic pride, saying "if you are a Turk you are happy." Under his leadership the new secular nation abolished polygamy and the wearing of veils, and gave women permission to vote.

Turkey is also rich in Christian history. All seven churches mentioned in the book of Revelation are located in Turkey, as well as many of the cities the apostle Paul visited on his missionary journeys. Visitors to Cappadocia can see hundreds of elaborately painted caves where believers lived and worshipped together.

Since Islam took hold, only a handful of Turks have followed Jesus, although this is changing. It is difficult to know for sure, but there may be as few as 500 Turkish believers in Turkey. Bible correspondence courses have brought more than half of these believers to Christ. Through such methods, Aysegul and her relatives may have the chance to hear the good news that has been kept from Turkish Muslims for hundreds of years.

Those who were not told about him will see, and those who have not heard will understand.
Romans 15:21

* Pray that new believers would be discipled and become active in winning others. Pray for the development of leaders for Turkish churches.

* Most Turkish believers are men. Pray for strategies to reach Turkish women as well.

* Though many Turks practice Islam only nominally, they consider it a strong part of their identity and say "to be Turkish is to be Muslim." Pray that Turks would find their identity in Christ.

* Ask God to open the eyes of Turks to himself as they study the New Testament through correspondence courses.

Qashqa'i

Homeland: Iran
Religion: Islam

In the mountains and deserts of south west Iran live a proud, nomadic people who have resisted attempts to absorb them into mainstream Iranian culture. The Qashqa'i call themselves Turks and speak a Turkic language similar to Azerbaijani. Though they are Shiah Muslims, most have little use for organised religion beyond political purposes. A traditionally nomadic way of life has kept the them from exposure to Christian witness. In 1996 there were no known Qashqa'i believers, churches, Bibles, or missionaries for them. This situation pricked the conscience of a few Christians who have begun to advocate for the needs of the Qashqa'i to the Christian community.

Thank you, Father, for these advocates and their desire for the Qashqa'i! Protect, provide for, and grant wisdom for the missionaries of many countries hoping to minister there.

Turkmen

Homeland:
    Turkmenistan, Iran,
    Afghanistan
Religion: Islam,
    Animism, Atheism

Legend has it that when God made the world, the Turkmen were first in line for sunshine and last in line for rain. Nomadic life in Central Asia's harsh Kara Kum desert was difficult, but allowed the Turkmen to maintain a society fairly independent of the kingdoms that claimed to rule them. Turkmen learned to depend only on their own families and tribes. Life today is different. "We do not think about the future much, because things are changing too rapidly," says Gulya, a young Turkmen woman. "Our nation is struggling to catch up with the modern world, while rediscovering our ancient heritage. Sometimes it makes me dizzy!" Gulya prefers the traditional life. She loves her job at the carpet factory, working and gossiping with other traditional women, elegant in their full-length embroidered dresses and colourful scarves. Since the fall of the Soviet Union in 1991, Turkmen national pride has grown. Many are embracing the Turkmen language, heritage, and culture once suppressed by the Soviets.

Lord, thank you for the hopeful future you have for the Turkmen people. Let many Turkmen come into your family, learn to depend on you, and follow your ways.

Azerbaijani

Homeland: Azerbaijan, Iran
Religion: Islam, Animism, Atheism

"Last year, I lent my Bible to a non-Christian friend," confides Elshad. "He had it for a long time, and though I was pleased he was so interested, I needed it back. Every time I asked for it, he put me off. Finally, I discovered the reason. He was hand-copying the entire book of Psalms! He told me that they were so poetic, and so beautiful, he just couldn't bear to part with them." The New Testament and a children's Bible are available in the Azerbaijani language, and a team of translators has begun work on the Old Testament. "We have a saying," explains one translator, "that someone who speaks the Azerbaijani language well sings like a nightingale. We desire this translation to sing to the hearts of our people." The middle-eastern heritage helps Turkic and Persian peoples understand the cultures and stories of the Bible.

Word of life, let translation projects in Turkic and Persian languages "sing to the hearts of the people."

Russia
Ukraine
Azerbaijan
Turk
Kazakstan
Turkmen
Azerbaijani-Afshari
Iran
Afghanistan
Qashqa'i
Saudi Arabia
Sudan

Yemeni Arabs

Homeland: Yemen
Religion: Islam

The groggy men suddenly came alive and cheered when the news came on the radio: "The civil war in Yemen is over. With help from Iran, Libya, and Sudan, the northern Islamic faction has defeated the south!"

"Do you think we will fight again?" Rayda asked his friend.

"Of course. We always have, and always will."

More than 16 million people live in Yemen, and 97 percent of them are Arab. Less than half a million people live in each of Yemen's two major cities, Sana'a and Aden. Yemen remains one of the poorest Arab countries. Frequently during the last three centuries the country has been divided into North and South. After independence from Britain in the 1960's and 1970's, North Yemen became a traditional Islamic state, and South Yemen, while home to primarily Muslim peoples as well, had a Soviet-backed Marxist government.

The two were united in 1990, but they are far from unified, and plagued by growing economic troubles. In 1994, less than a year after their first democratic elections, a short civil war rocked the nation. Today the disunity of the country's 1,700 clans and tribes threaten the uneasy peace. In the past these tribesmen were under the rule of *imams*, the Islamic spiritual and temporal rulers. Each man could bring the smallest problem directly to this leader and speak with him face to face. This may be one reason Yemeni people resist political hierarchy.

Almost 100 percent of Yemenis are Muslims, although they are not united in this. Those in the south and centre are Sunni, while Shiites live in the northeast. Yemeni women lead restricted lives, and many are kept secluded in their homes. In Yemen, as in most Arab countries, Christian missionaries are excluded. The only Christians from abroad allowed into the country are those who have marketable skills in secular jobs. Most of these Christian workers were evacuated during the civil war, but the majority have now returned and re-established their witness in Yemen.

Blessed are the poor in spirit, for theirs is the kingdom of heaven.
Matthew 5:3

• By mid-afternoon on any given day many men are semi-drugged from chewing a narcotic weed called *qat*. Qat's use is so extensive that the road system in Yemen was designed and built around the most efficient way to get qat from the fields into the cities. Pray that God would rescue Yemenis from this physical bondage.

• Pray that God would call, equip, and send many Christians from around the world to minister in Yemen.

• Pray for increased government openness for Christians, so that expatriate Christians might continue their work in Yemen.

• Pray for the translation of the Bible into the Yemeni Arabic dialect and for cassette tapes of this translation.

Bedouin

Homeland: Saudi Arabia, North Africa
Religion: Islam

Numerous Arabic-speaking nomadic tribes roam the deserts from the Atlantic coast of North Africa to Jordan and Iraq. Originally from the Arabian Peninsula, present day Saudi Arabia, they spread throughout the Middle East and North Africa as the "warriors of Islam." Today many Saudi Arabians are Bedouins who have become incredibly wealthy in the oil industry, but others maintain their simple lifestyle. Bedouin life is governed by a fierce code of ethics which includes loyalty to one's clan and tribe, hospitality to strangers (even enemies), and blood vengeance on those who kill one of your clan. The Bedouin are paradoxically both looked down upon by other Arabs for their lack of sophistication, and admired for the Muslim virtues expressed in their ethical code. To introduce Bedouins to Christ in a relevant and meaningful way will take patience and creativity. Recent governmental attempts to forcibly settle these nomadic people have introduced tremendous stresses and changes into their traditional world view.

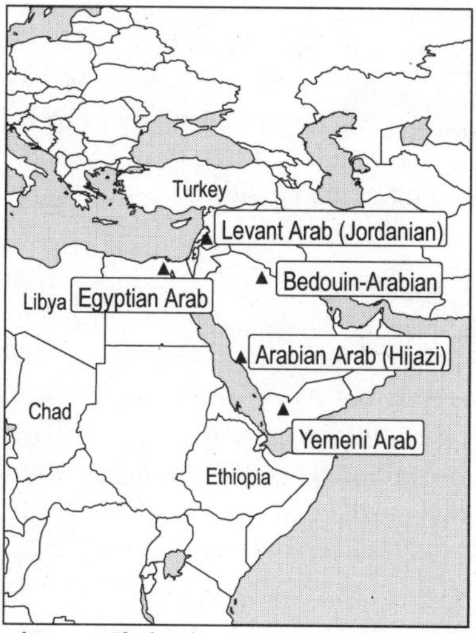

Holy God, you care for strangers and foreigners. Extend your love and grace to the Bedouin.

Levant Arabs

Homeland: Syria, Iraq, Jordan, Lebanon
Religion: Islam

The part of Syria and Lebanon called the Levant is one of the few places in the world where Muslims and Christians live and work side by side, speaking the same language and, until recently, living in peace. Syria and Lebanon are Arab countries, and Arabic is their official language. Both countries have large, respected Christian populations. In spite of this, a long tradition makes it difficult for many Christians to see their Muslim neighbours as people to whom they can minister and introduce Christ. Christians minister and evangelise freely within their own communities, but the government actively discourages any attempts to minister to Muslims.

Jesus, fill our brothers and sisters so full of your love that they can not help but share with their Muslim neighbours, friends, and coworkers.

Egyptian Arabs

Homeland: Egypt
Religion: Islam

Egypt is another predominantly Arabic-speaking Muslim land with an ancient Christian minority. Nearly one fifth of the Egyptian population calls itself Christian, whether Coptic, Catholic, or Protestant. However, the Christians make up 75 percent of the population emigrating to the West. Urban populations in Egypt are swelling, especially in Cairo, and the consequent masses of young unemployed men make fertile soil for Islamic militant groups. Anwar Sadat, Egypt's late president, courageously defied the conventional wisdom of his time. Under his leadership, Egypt was the first Arab state to seek a peace treaty with Israel. Because of this, he was assassinated. Militant groups have fought an underground guerrilla war against the current government. Only Christ can bring true and lasting peace to Egypt.

Prince of peace, call many of our Egyptian brothers and sisters to stay and reach out to Muslims with compassion and humility. Show us what we can do to help them do this.

Map labels: Turkey, Levant Arab (Jordanian), Bedouin-Arabian, Libya, Egyptian Arab, Arabian Arab (Hijazi), Chad, Yemeni Arab, Ethiopia

Maghreb Arabs

Homeland: Algeria, Morocco, Tunisia, France
Religion: Islam

Eighteen-year-old Salaam was driving. His cousin, Ibraham, 17, was gawking out of the passenger's window of Salaam's battered Toyota. It was a warm, sunny day and the idle young men were enjoying the smells and sights of the open market, hoping as they drove out of town to catch a glimpse of the young women who sometimes shopped at this market. They were heading to one of their favourite haunts in the desert. They brought provisions to keep them for several days, but they really did not know how long they would stay. Unemployed and out of school, Salaam and Ibraham had no responsibilities that required their return. Neither had a family, as they could not marry without good jobs to support their children.

The paved, two-lane road that took them away from town enabled them to increase their speed considerably. Periodically, Salaam swerved sharply to avoid oncoming traffic. Often the other cars on the road would also need to make quick and strong adjustments to avoid collisions. Each time this happened, Sallam and Ibraham would breathe, "in shaa al-laah" (as God wills). As they had been taught, they believed their actions did not really matter that much. Their lives were in Allah's hands.

The Maghreb Arabs have been Muslim for generations. A portion of the early church, and several of our well-known church fathers like Augustine, lived in North Africa, but today little is left of this church. Protestant missions have only been active in this part of the world over the last hundred years. Small groups of believers meet together in homes across North Africa, but many believers are isolated and have no chance to meet other believers. The laws of these Islamic countries often forbid evangelism and conversion.

Church growth is very slow, needing much support from outside, as well as from tentmakers living inside the countries. Some parts of North Africa have never had any Protestant missionaries. In other countries it has only been during the past several years that people have started trusting Christ.

From the west, men will fear the name of the LORD, and from the rising of the sun, they will revere his glory. Isaiah 59:19a

- Islam has created a kind of fatalism within the Arab cultures. Pray that Arabs would be attracted to the Creator God, who is concerned about their lives.

- Forty-two percent of the Maghreb are under 15 years of age, yet there are no ministries reaching out to these children. Pray for creative ministries to reach the next generation with the good news.

- Unemployment is a problem in all the countries where these people live, reaching up to 40 percent. Pray that young people would not be discouraged and would find creative work to do.

- Thank the Lord for an openness for the gospel in the lives of many. Pray that they would meet their Saviour.

Libyan Arabs

Homeland: Libya
Religion: Islam

"The crises facing the Muslim world are home grown, developed through decades of deprivation, with the political structures in these countries failing to provide any democratic outlets that could lead to a semblance of justice." (*Muslim News, 22-12-95*) Nowhere is this more true than in Libya. Mu'ammar Ghadaffi led a military coup in 1969 and has remained in control ever since. He tolerates no dissent. No open evangelism is possible and that has effectively limited the growth of the church. Few Christians have been able to enter Libya with the intention of sharing the gospel with Arabs, although several radio stations beam evangelical programs there. Libyan Arabs form nearly 80 percent of the country's population. These Arabs have very little or no opportunity to hear of Jesus' love and the hope of eternal life in him.

King of kings, raise up a just and open government in Libya.

Hassaniya Arabs

Homeland: Mauritania, Morocco
Religion: Islam

The Hassinaya Arabs, also known as Moors, were born from the union of Arabs and Berber cultures in northwest Africa. They built a flourishing empire on the profit of their camel caravans, trading in gold and eventually slaves. The Hassaniya no longer flourish. Their homeland, Mauritania, ranks 18th on the Index of Human Suffering. The Hassaniya have a low life expectancy and high infant mortality rate. Slightly more than half of their school-age children attend primary school. Less than 20 percent of the population is literate. The slave trade continues, unofficially, giving Mauritania the dubious distinction of having the largest number of slaves in the world, between 5 and 10 percent of the population. The Hassaniya Arabs are among the poorest of the poor.

Spirit, be poured out as in Isaiah 32 so the desert peoples of the western Sahara could become like your garden.

Sudan Arabs

Homeland: Sudan
Religion: Islam

Converting to Christianity is a crime in the Sudan; a policy enforced brutally. Government harassment leaves believers three options: convert to Islam, flee, or be killed. Christian families have lost thousands of children who have been snatched and sold as slaves to buyers in Sudan, Libya, and other Islamic countries. Thousands of women have been raped and sold as servants or concubines. There are even reports of men being crucified. Sudanese Arabs make up only a third of the country's population; nevertheless, they hold tight control of the government and economy. Even though the government's stability is bolstered by massive aid from Libya and Iran, the price of power has been high. Sudan is a country divided; the economy is devastated. In spite of tremendous natural resources, most of the people are very poor.

God of the martyrs, let the Sudanese Christians provide a powerful and attractive testimony to the Muslim Arabs who seek to destroy them.

Riff Berber

Homeland: Northern Morocco
Religion: Sunni Islam,
Animism, Sufism

Even after six months in France, Ahmed felt dwarfed by Casablanca's high-rises and minarets. Merchants vied to show him their wares. Ragged children and idle young men filled the streets. Grandmothers in their veils shared the sidewalks with fashionable young ladies in high heels. Adobe houses stood in the shade of tall concrete buildings. "It's good to be back in Morocco," Ahmed thought, "but I don't belong in the city." Home was several days' trek farther, a village high in the Riff mountains where his family waited.

Life in the mountains has not changed much. While centuries of foreign invasions took the coastlands, Berbers found refuge in the rugged mountains and deserts where they could speak their own languages, following their own laws and customs undisturbed. Ahmed identifies primarily with his family and tribe. His family is Muslim, but keeps practices more ancient than Islam. One of Ahmed's cousins is a "marabout," a holy man who practices healing and casts out evil spirits. Most local problems never make it to government officials, but are solved by tribal elders.

Fatima knew the family needed the money Ahmed brought back from his work in France. She poured strong mint tea from the steaming pot, then sat back to listen to him talk. Fatima missed her husband, but had a busy life of her own. The lives of Berber men and women seldom overlap. When she wants to talk, Fatima goes to her neighbours, who are mostly relatives.

Ascribe to the LORD, O families of nations, ascribe to the LORD glory and strength. Psalm 96:7

• Hundreds of thousands of Riff Berbers live in Europe. Others, like Ahmed, travel back and forth to Europe for work. Pray for ministry to Berbers in Europe, who might be more open to hear the gospel and be influencial in the Riff region.

• There were Berber churches in early Christian history but when Islam came, they crumbled. Pray for the birth of new Berber churches which reflect a value for Berber culture and identity.

• Thank God for the popularity of the *Jesus* film, being copied and distributed by Berbers who are proud of the only movie in their own language. Pray for its effectiveness in reaching them.

• Raising hashish, a narcotic, is a major source of income for Riff Berbers. Pray for Christian organisations to provide people with job options as an alternative to this drug trade.

Tamazight Berber

Homeland: Morocco, Algeria
Religion: Islam, Animism

Once nomads, many Tamazight-speaking Berbers (also known as the Central Shilha Berbers) still leave their villages in the summer to follow their herds through the Middle Atlas mountains. The three million Tamazight-speaking Berbers call themselves *Imazighen*, "the free." They are intensely loyal to family and clan, and call each member of their tribe, "cousin." More frequently than other Muslim groups, Berbers offer animal sacrifices to earn blessing for their families, tribes, and herds.

Father, bring the Tamazight Berbers eternal blessing through the blood of your son.

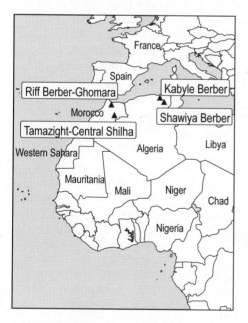

Kabyle Berber

Homeland: Algeria
Religion: Islam, Animism

The Kabyle village sits perched on a mountain ridge, stone houses with red tile roofs overlooking endless terraces of farmland spread out below. Until the arrival of the French in the 19th century, the Kabyle homeland in Algeria had never been ruled by a foreign power. Yet God is not foreign and can not be held off by the impenetrable mountains. Praise God for several thousands of Kabyle Berbers who have turned to Christ recently. Pray for the Kayble Christian leaders, some of whose lives are in danger in this largely Muslim country.

Spirit, strengthen and encourage Kabyle Berbers and establish your church among them, that they might reach those who have no church at all.

Shawiya Berber

Homeland: Algeria
Religion: Islam, Animism

Tall stone grain silos dot the Shawiya landscape. Along with a mosque and a gathering place for men, the silo forms the heart of a small Shawiya village. The silo represents the tribe's wealth, the gathering place its wisdom, and the mosque its power. Ancestors may be buried in this village centre, their tombs the source of blessing and protection for the whole community. Both men and women seek and practice magic. Some Shawiya literature claims that all women are magicians, learning incantations and potions from their mothers.

Mighty God, demonstrate your power and reveal your mercy for the Shawiya.

Tuareg

Homeland: Niger, Mali, Burkina Faso
Religion: Islam, Animism

Photo Courtesy Bernice Condit.

The sun sets in the desert. An elegant woman sings in a high voice, accompanying herself on her *anzad,* an instrument with a single string. Men and women sit around the campfire, quiet, listening with respect. Her melody is hauntingly beautiful, like the Saharan night. Such songs date back to a time, centuries ago when the Tuareg ruled the desert. Now, as then, women pass down tribal traditions by teaching their daughters poetry and music.

An aura of mystery surrounds the desert nomads known as the Tuareg. All of their adult life, the tall, fair Tuareg men cover themselves with a long blue veil, which the most conservative will not remove in front of others even to eat. Long known as warriors, traders, and capable guides through the dangers of the Sahara desert, the Tuareg find their independence now threatened as drought after drought kills their herds. Like so many others, they are pushed south as the desert expands. Many have been forced to give up their nomadic lifestyle and move to the cities for work. As they leave the desert, many leave behind their age-old way of life.

The Tuareg have a rigid caste system, but unlike their Arab neighbours, they balance the responsibilities of men and women. Tuareg women, the guardians of language, are often asked to decide questions of law or literature. Tuareg children inherit their mother's property and social status, even into marriage.

Tuareg means "the forsaken of God," a name given them by the Arabs, though, the Tuareg refer to themselves simply as "the free men." Their nomadic tradition gives them independence to respect neither political nor religious authority. While the Tuareg are nominally Muslim, many came to the desert to avoid submitting to Arab conquerors and converting to Islam. They use music to cast out evil spirits, and amulets to protect themselves from lonely spirits haunting the desert. Many Tuareg, especially those who have left nomadic life for the city, admit that they too are a lonely people.

Now the dwelling of God is with men, and he will live with them. They will be his people, and God himself will be with them and be their God.
Revelation 21:3b

♦ For generations the Tuareg have been proud and independent, but now their way of life is being challenged. Pray for Christians who can address their physical and spiritual needs.

♦ Pray that the Holy Spirit would inspire Tuareg music and literature, rightly recounting the story of Jesus' life.

♦ High-caste Tuareg are light-skinned and look down on people with darker skin, including many neighbouring peoples. Pray they might receive the gospel from those they respect, yet come to see that the Creator God loves all races.

♦ Many Tuareg now live in cities, but most are poor and illiterate and cannot find work. Pray for literacy and development programs among them.

Saharan Berber

Homeland: Algeria
Religion: Islam, Animism

Centuries ago several groups of Berbers, persecuted for their strict form of Islam, migrated from northern Algeria to an area south of Algiers. Their homeland may be the most desolate region of the Sahara. One of the groups, the Mzabi, built five cities on the slope of the Wadi Mzab, a river that flows only once every dozen years. In the holy city Beni-Isguen, strangers are not allowed to stay the night. The Mzabis have the distinction of being the only city-dwelling people of the Sahara, but must work constantly to irrigate their elaborate network of palm groves and gardens. Mzabis do not marry outside their community, nor allow outsiders to enter their mosques. Mzabi men travel all over Algeria working as shop keepers and running small businesses, but women stay in the oasis.

Holy Spirit, bring streams of living water to the Mzabis and other Berber groups of the desert.

Southern Shilha Berber

Homeland: Morocco, Algeria
Religion: Islam, Animism

Several million Shilha, or Isilhayn Berbers live in Morocco's high Atlas mountains, where they inhabit deep river valleys. Their small, isolated villages often lay close to the river, with mountain slopes above divided into pasture and farmland. Some of the storehouses forming the focus of Southern Shilha communities were built by ancestors in the 17th and 18th centuries. Many Southern Shilha are leaving their villages to seek better jobs in Morocco's northern cities. After securing jobs, workers live frugally and send money home until their families can join them. Some of these city Shilha have come into contact with small groups of Arab and expatriate Christians. A few have become believers, but they have no church to call their own.

Lord, bring lasting fruit from radio broadcasts to isolated mountain people like the Shilha.

Shuwa Arabs

Homeland: Chad, Sudan, Nigeria, Niger
Religion: Islam, Animism

"My greatest success is my family," says the Shuwa Arab patriarch. "Every night my sons and grandsons return to my tents with the herds, my heart swells with pride. Nothing could be worse than the barren, impoverished home, anonymous with no sons to pass down the name." As a people, the Shuwa Arabs are far from anonymous. Indeed, they may be the most influential of Chad's peoples. Chadian Arab groups are scattered across Chad from east to west. Living in close contact with all the country's people groups, Arabs visit the markets of the Sahel, marry the daughters of other tribes and sometimes share their way of life. When cultures meet, however, it is the Arabic culture that has sway. Their language is used in government, religion, and literature, and was for many centuries the only written language of Chad.

Christ, may Arab traders spread your good name through the Sahel, as they spread Islam so many years ago.

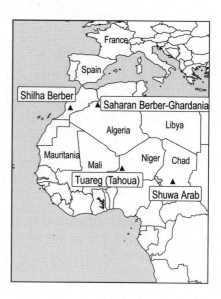

- 77 -

Somali

Homeland: Somalia, Ethiopia
Religion: Islam

Photo Courtesy FMB.

Somali children giggle as they watch their mother try to milk the stubborn goat. Among the ten million Somali nomads and farmers of north east Africa, women and young children care for sheep and goats, while the young men and boys are responsible for herding the highly esteemed camels. In a land that has an average rainfall of less than four inches a year, the Somalis' lives are consumed with finding water and grazing land for their livestock.

Children are taught history and tradition through poetry. The Somalis have remarkable memories and often chant folk tales to entertain themselves on long night walks. The gospel is most clear to them when it is presented in Biblical poetic stories. Although portions of Scripture are available in their language, few Somali are literate. Radio broadcasts and taped Christian messages are more useful.

Modern life in the city of Mogadishu is ravaged by clan rivalry. No one cares if a member of another clan starves. As many as 30,000 automatic weapons are held by men and boys who steal food meant for the relief of those who are starving. Some of them sell the food to support their drug habit of chewing narcotic *qat* leaves. Relief agencies continue trying to distribute food and medical supplies to the needy.

Ninety-eight percent of the 7.5 million people of Somalia are Somali and 99 percent are Muslim. Somali Christians are despised. Drought, famine, and war have driven many from their homes to surrounding countries. Somali refugees in Kenya, where there is complete religious freedom, are showing increasing interest in Christianity. Those who flee to Yemen and Ethiopia, however, only face more war, poverty, and clan rivalry.

He tends his flock like a shepherd: he gathers the lambs in his arms and carries them close to his heart. Isaiah 40:11a

- Pray for the Kenyan Somalis to turn to Christ and carry the message to the Somalis in Somalia and Ethiopia.

- Pray that God would bless the work of World Vision, SIM, and other agencies attempting to penetrate this unreached people group with the gospel.

- As cultural change challenges the Somalis' traditional way of life, pray they would embrace the truth of Jesus.

- Pray God would bring relief to the Somali refugees' great affliction and show them his salvation.

Afar

Homeland: Somalia, Ethiopia
Religion: Islam, Animist

A virtuous Afar man is tough, warlike, and quick to take revenge. The strikingly beautiful Afar women will not even consider a courtship with one who has never killed another man. They hope for a husband who wears the iron bracelet indicating that he has killed ten men. Unemployment, illiteracy, and violence plague this Muslim tribe of Ethiopian origin. The Afar pack their portable houses on the backs of camels over what has been called "the most inhospitable desert in the world." They harvest salt to trade with coastal peoples in Djibouti and Eritrea. Afars living in Djibouti have a greater chance of hearing the gospel. Reaching the Afar and other peoples in the Horn of Africa requires mainly oral presentations of the gospel.

Holy Spirit, create a desire and thirst within the Afar to know the truth and worship you.

Beja

Homeland: Sudan, Egypt, Eritrea
Religion: Islam, Animist

Although many of the nomadic Beja are hostile toward Christianity, in recent months a few Beja started following Jesus. Traditional Beja beliefs mix Islam with fear of *jinn*, or evil spirits. However, a response to the gospel is growing slowly. The Beja are divided into five major tribes and many smaller subtribes, speaking several languages. This makes it difficult for Christian workers to communicate the gospel with them effectively. Nevertheless, there may be as many as a dozen baptised Beja believers today, and one man is preparing to translate the Bible into To-Bedawie, the chief Beja language. Of course, 12 Christians among 2.5 million Beja still leaves room for growth.

Father, bless and protect these few Beja believers and work through the Bible translation project to set the Beja free to serve you.

Nubian

Homeland: Egypt, Sudan
Religion: Animist

As Sudan's Islamic government seizes Nubian property and sells it to Arabic-speaking Muslims nearby, the distinctive Nubian culture is fading away. Their villages are being destroyed and their children sold into slavery. Nubians disagree about why their people are dying. Some say it is because they have no more cattle to sacrifice to the spirits. Some say God has abandoned them because they expelled the Christian priests.

Jesus, let the Nubians know you have not abandoned them, and open the doors of opportunity for them to hear your message of love.

Photo Courtesy Bernice Condit.

Peoples of the Sahel

Homeland: Chad, Nigeria, Niger, Sudan
Religion: Islam, Animism

Hundreds of small tribes live in the African Sahel, on the southern fringe of the great Sahara desert. Their massive numbers represent a great challenge for the church, and a call for cross-cultural pioneers. The Teda are one of these Sahel peoples.

Every year the desert expands and the Teda elder Fodul must take his family and herds farther south to reach the grasslands, and dig his wells deeper to get precious water, until at last the fragile walls collapse inward. Some rich Teda families have horses and camels, but even these cannot survive without water.

"There is no more grass for our sheep and cattle," Fodul tells his children. "The clan must move on."

Many Teda people live in the same small villages year round, but some, like Fodul, migrate for the survival of their herds. Fodul lives in the northern reaches of Chad, one of the driest places on earth. He and his family are among more than 400,000 Teda tribesmen living in Niger, Chad, Sudan, and Libya.

Like many nomadic and semi-nomadic people groups, the Teda have little meaningful contact or identification with people outside their own clan or tribe. Though the number of languages is great, the number of tribes is still greater. The Daza, the Zaghawa, the Bideyat—these people groups live similar but separate lives and will have to come to know God through separate efforts.

Churches for every people group in the Sahel? The task seems too complex, the peoples too diverse and too remote, but what a day of glory it will be when God is worshipped in the Sahel by members of every tribe and in hundreds of languages!

You, O Lord, are a compassionate and gracious God, slow to anger, abounding in love and faithfulness. Psalm 86:15

> • The Teda and other peoples of the Sahel are dependent on a fragile environment. Pray that many would seek God as the Earth's powerful creator who can meet all their needs.
>
> • Pray for peace among the Sahelian tribes as they compete for fewer resources.
>
> • Pray for a multitude of church planters, Bible translators and development workers willing to minister in Jesus' name to the many small tribes of this difficult region.
>
> • Pray that the Holy Spirit would prepare the hearts of the Sahelian people to receive the gospel of Jesus Christ.

Fur

Homeland: Sudan
Religion: Animism, some Islam

The laughter and chatter of women and children fills the air on market day. Women exchange news as they compare prices on tomatoes and millet. Nearby, their sons and husbands gather to raise a new house for a family in their village. Each one brings wood for beams or grass for the thatched roof. In return, the owner of the new house provides beer that one of his wives has brewed. Above the village stretch terraced fields, their crops nourished by rich volcanic soil. Husbands and wives raise their crops separately, maintaining some economic independence. More than 700,000 Fur people live in western Sudan, yet they have no Bible, radio broadcasts, gospel recordings, relief work, or missionaries.

Lamb of God, call forth labourers for a harvest among the Fur who will certainly not be left out of the marriage feast.

Chadic

Homeland: Nigeria, Chad, Sudan
Religion: Animism, Islam

Missionaries first entered the Goemei area in 1907 and were predominantly Roman Catholics. Today there are churches from all major Protestant denominations plus the Jehovah's Witnesses. The Hausa language is used in all church services in the towns and rural villages, but there are also a few English services. There is no translation of Scripture in the Goemei language. Until the 1960's, services were held in Goemei, but this was discontinued when the government took over the mission schools and pushed toward Hausa and English as languages to unify the country. Because of intermarriage and ethnic mixing in towns, there are Goemei attending a variety of churches. These few Goemei Christians consider the Catholic church their mother church. There are a few Muslims among the Goemei, but traditional religion is more common. Even Christians often revert to traditional rites when faced with life problems. This is recognised as a serious problem by the Catholic church.

Spirit, would you send a profound awakening among the Goemei believers that they would know you truly and deeply. Also, inspire the two Goemei laymen who are receiving training to work on a Goemei Bible.

Masalit

Homeland: Sudan, Chad
Religion: Islam, Animism

The 250,000 Masalit of Sudan and Chad are nominally Muslim, but they intersperse their Friday prayers in the village mosque with prayers to the spirits of the land and sky. The Masalit are often very poor, living in mud huts and surviving by subsistence farming. Few can read or write in French or Arabic, the national languages of their countries, and their own language, Masalit, is unwritten.

Lord of life, help the Masalit prosper as a people. Bless Bible translators attempting to bring your good news to the Masalit.

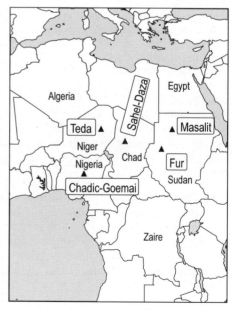

Fulani

Photo Courtesy Christian Reformed World Missions.

Homeland: Nigeria, Senegal, Guinea, Mali, Burkina Faso, Niger, Chad, Cameroon
Religion: Islam

Many Fulani live lives that have changed little in more than a millennium. The nomadic Fulani, or Fulbe, as they prefer to be called, remain cattle herders, living simply and in complete harmony with their environment. Only twice has the outside world forced the Fulani to look beyond their herds to confront change. About 200 years ago Islam came. Some Fulani became Muslims voluntarily, and the rest were forced to convert at the point of a sword. The second change came about 100 years later, when the French came to northwest Africa. They brought a different culture, different form of government, and different attitudes toward nature. They brought the plough, vehicles, and coin money. The Fulani resisted as best they could, but change was inevitable.

In the 1980's some Americans moved into Fulani villages. These western Christians have begun reaching out to the Fulani, especially during times of famine. Many Fulani are hearing the gospel for the first time. The villagers do not yet know that this message will bring change greater than any they have yet encountered. It will be profound and inescapable. Eventually every Fulani will choose.

Dayibu has already made his decision, and become a Christian...secretly...afraid to learn more or be found out. His neighbour, Habbi, has made no decision, but is investigating from afar. The son of their *imam* (Muslim teacher) has begun to research Christianity publicly, but seems untouched for now. Several Fulani families have turned to Christ and are reaching out to their fellow tribesmen.

Many Fulani find the man Jesus attractive, but they are uncertain, concerned for what might lay ahead. Watching the lives of the white people who pray in the name of Jesus, they debate, reflect, talk, and wonder. Would life be better under Christianity than Islam? Are the promises of salvation really true? How can they know?

**"Not by might nor by power, but by my Spirit," says the LORD Almighty.
Zechariah 4:6b**

• Pray that Fulani throughout West Africa would be willing and able to choose the positive change that salvation in Christ would bring, redeeming their culture for God's purposes.

• Pray for the destruction of the barrier of fear that grips many who would choose Christ.

• Pray for the few Christian Fulani to witness boldly for Christ. Also pray for Christian workers to be raised up to minister the truth to the Fulani.

• Pray that the use of cassettes, film, and other technologies would advance the gospel among the millions of Fulani in West Africa.

Wolof

Homeland: Senegal, Gambia
Religion: Islam, Animism

The Wolof of Senegal number three million, but less than 200 are believers—even after years of Christian witness among them. More than 90 percent are Muslim, but many still believe real power comes from contact with the spirit world, so they wear *gre-gris*, charms filled with verses from the Koran. The ministry of Christians providing food, medical help, and water development, as well as the publication of a Wolof New Testament in 1987, has brought increased openness and interest in the gospel.

Lord Jesus, thank you for opening the hearts of many Wolof people to your gift of salvation. Break the bonds of Islam and spirit worship and use your people and your word to bring many more Wolof to yourself.

Fon

Homeland: Benin
Religion: Animism

The Fon of Benin have good reason to rejoice! The Fon language New Testament is now complete, and the Old Testament is well on the way. The members of the two dozen Fon churches can now study God's word in their own language. Though well educated, the Fon have long been in bondage to Animism and the use of fetishes. It was in Benin that the voodoo religion began, spreading to places like Haiti through the slave trade. The Old Testament will be significant because it teaches animistic peoples like the Fon to avoid idolatry and worship only the one, true God.

Jesus, we pray that you would continue to build your church among the Fon people. Help believers to grow in their understanding of who you are through your word. Free them to fully comprehend your love and grace.

Gur

Homeland: Mali, Togo, Burkina Faso, Ghana
Religion: Mainly Animism

Firecrackers exploded in the air. Men blew whistles and smiling women swayed back and forth around the swaddled corpse. This was done in hope of pleasing the ancestors. Ousman, a young Senoufo boy, was attending his first funeral. One of the Gur peoples, the Senoufo of West Africa number more than 2.2 million and live in Cote d'Ivoire, Mali, and Burkina Faso. Senoufos are primarily farmers, with much of their mythology associated with the earth. Their animistic rituals honour ancestral and nature spirits. Strong communal values have resisted both Islam and Christianity. Senoufo carved masks and amulets are world famous and can be found in Western museums.

King of glory, open the hearts of the Senoufo to know you as their Saviour. Draw entire villages to your throne of grace.

- 83 -

Malinke

Homeland: West Africa
Religion: Islam, Animism

Photo Courtesy Bob Fetherlin, Christian & Missionary Alliance.

Gadiri's eyes sparkled as he ran toward the place from where the music was coming. How he loved to hear the minstrel sing the legend of the Lion King, who founded Mali in the early 13th century. Because of his exploits, the Mandingo language, economic influence, and social system spread many miles in every direction. Though large, the Malinke are only one of many Mandingo peoples spread throughout West Africa. Famous as traders, the Mandingo peoples are also responsible for bringing Islam to sub-Saharan Africa.

More than half of the seven million Malinke can be found in the two countries of Mali and Guinea. Many live in remote villages that are not accessible by roads. Tribal members sometimes find it difficult to relate to one another because groups are separated by hundreds of miles. Not only are tribes scattered long distances, they are often isolated from facilities like schools and hospitals.

When the Malinke first become ill, they call on spirits for protection and healing. Islamic holy men in the villages say special prayers and give advice. Medicine is sought only when these fetishes and incantations have failed.

Last year, Gadiri's father and mother travelled over 100 kilometres to visit a medical clinic at Kenieba, Mali. There, they received medicine needed for dysentery. Missionaries at the hospital invited Gadiri's parents to listen to a recording about Jesus, a man from God who had power to heal the sick. Gadiri's parents invited anyone from the clinic to come to their village, but no one came. Perhaps the trip was too difficult to make.

Heal me, O LORD, and I will be healed; save me and I will be saved, for you are the one I praise.
Jeremiah 17:14

• The spirits who live among the Malinke do not want men, women, and children like Gadiri and his family to give worship to Jesus Christ. Pray for the spiritual release of the these people.

• Pray for the Malinke of Europe. Due to drought and economic hardship, many have left Africa to live in France. Without prestige and influence they must adapt to European life and try their best to make a living and support their families remaining in West Africa.

• Some of the missionaries to the Malinke have been forced to leave their work because of sickness and lack of adequate facilities. Pray for their health and strength.

• Ask God to open doors for the gospel to be presented in stories and other forms the Malinke appreciate.

Soninke

Homeland: Mali, Senegal, Cote d'Ivoire
Religion: Islam, Animism

More than a million West Africans living in six countries belong to the Soninke or Sarakole group of peoples, although many speak the languages of surrounding tribes. Converted to Islam in the 11th century, these Muslims have been active in propagating their religion. Today many of West Africa's most learned Islamic scholars are Soninke. The average Soninke villager is highly aware of spiritual forces, which he seeks to control through a complex system of charms and spells, relying also on the protection of the Muslim saint appointed as his spiritual guardian on the day he was named. Like so many other West African peoples living on the Sahara's fragile edge, the Soninke are slowly migrating south to find fertile land. Many young men travel to European cities like Paris, where they work as dishwashers or manual labourers and earn money to send home to their families.

Lord Jesus, speed the day when many Soninke worship you and boldly teach your truth.

Susu

Homeland: Guinea, Sierra Leone
Religion: Islam, Animism

Most of the nearly one million Susu people live in Guinea, West Africa, where they comprise ten percent of the population. The rest, in Sierra Leone, are not far away. Close-knit Susu villagers work together to fish, produce salt, grow rice, pineapples, mangoes, and coconuts. Most children, busy helping their parents with the harvest, have no time to attend school. Several ministry efforts have sparked a desire for the Bible in the Susu language, but many Susu are illiterate.

Christ, help the several churches who have "adopted" the Susu, committing to pray faithfully for them until growing churches exist among them.

Dioula

Homeland: Cote d'Ivoire, Burkina Faso
Religion: Islam, Animism

Mamadou sits on the river bank, looking across the water to the lush forests on the other side. His family has lived by this river, in Cote d'Ivoire, for many generations, but today his only son leaves for the city where he will study at the university. Mamadou wonders if village life will have any attraction for the boy once he experiences life in the modern city. Traditionally the strength of Dioula society is the family. A man can take as many as five wives; the children they bear him are the only security he has against the difficulties of old age. He trains his sons in the secrets of his own trade, that they may be able to care for him when he is old. Today more Dioula are going to school or moving away from their families to pursue careers in the city. Family no longer plays the role it once did. Many young Dioula are looking to money for security instead. Others hope that Islamic fundamentalism or a revival of traditional religions will restore stability to their society.

Father, give the Dioula the hope of the gospel and bring many of them into your eternal family!

Photo Courtesy Christian Reformed World Missions.

Hausa

Homeland: Nigeria, Niger
Religion: Islam, Animism

You begin your journey flying over the vast swamps of the Nigerian coast, where river banks are obscured by the twisted root of mangrove trees. Where the swamp ends, the forest begins. As you travel north the climate is hotter and drier. Approaching the Sahara you see bushes and shrubs growing in coarse grass, and fewer trees. North of the savannah country, the only vegetation is rough grass, and beyond that lies the desert. Here, on the edge of the great desert, is the city of Kano.

Because it seldom rains in this ancient Hausa city, the dried clay houses have flat roofs. The oldest part of Kano is surrounded by an immense wall with 13 gates. The slender white turrets of a mosque rise above the brown houses. Kano is the biggest town on the southern edge of the Sahara and a gateway to the desert. For generations past, caravans came through Kano with their loads of ivory, gold and slaves.

A young Hausa boy, Bala, lives in a compound just inside the walls. He shares a house with his mother, brothers, and sisters. His father and uncles live in another house, and his father's other wives and children are nearby. Because divorce is common in Hausa society, Bala has changed fathers twice during his childhood, and has known many stepsisters and stepbrothers. His father and uncles make indigo cloth and travel across Africa selling it. They love to bargain, haggling for hours over prices, but when a deal is agreed they are steadfast and faithful.

Bala and his family are among 30 million Hausa-speakers, whose communities stretch across North and West Africa. More than 20 million of them live in Nigeria alone. The physical contrast between Nigeria's lush south and arid north is matched by a spiritual contrast. Although Nigerian churches are active in world evangelisation, historic friction makes reaching the Muslim northerners of their own country difficult. The complete Bible is available in Nigerian Hausa, but many Hausa cannot read.

Oh, that their hearts would be inclined to fear me and keep all my commands always, so that it might go well with them and their children forever! Deuteronomy 5:29

• Ask God to protect and defend children like Bala, to nurture and draw them to himself, that they might lead others.

• The Hausa seem open to hear the gospel, but resistant to religious change. Ask God to grant them repentance and conviction about the gospel's significance.

• Pray for the physical needs of Hausa in Niger and Nigeria. Severe famines have brought more openness for the gospel, as missionaries provided compassionate help.

• Praise God for a Hausa Bible school. May it equip Hausa believers to lead, and to cross cultural borders and share with unreached people groups around them.

Swahili

Homeland: Tanzania, Kenya, throughout
East Africa
Religion: Islam

Twelve centuries ago Arab merchants settled
on the coastal strip and small coral islands
of eastern Africa, intermarrying with people
there and bringing their culture and religion
with them. Swahili, a Bantu language with
many Arabic words, is one of the most widely
spoken in all of Africa. Nearly all Swahili-
speaking peoples are Muslim. Many are
devout, organising their daily routine by the
five prayer times announced by the mosque
callers. Others practice Islam only nominally,
but agree with their more orthodox friends
that Christianity is an immoral religion. This
view is only bolstered by contacts they have
with tourists who come to visit their areas.
Although Swahili speakers welcome outsiders, 12 centuries of practising Islam make it
difficult to consider converting to Christianity. Thousands of missionaries work in Kenya
and Tanzania, but in Swahili speaking areas
few focus on the Muslim peoples.

*Jesus, use your church to show Swahili-
speaking Muslims the true nature of grace
and righteousness.*

Songhai

Homeland: Mali, Niger
Religion: Islam, Animism

About four million Muslim Songhai live in
scattered towns and villages along the Niger
River in West Africa. Islam has slightly affected the deeply rooted Animism of their
ancient culture, which focuses instead on
the reverence of spiritual forces that govern
the elements—the soil, the river, and their
crops. Once a powerful people, the Songhai
have watched their world shrink as the advancing Sahara desert swallows village after
village. Relief and development workers in
Songhai areas have helped the Songhai
adapt to this changing climate. Such work
can give a good name to the gospel and open
Songhai hearts to God.

*Lord, use Christian relief workers to show
the Songhai your eternal kingdom.*

Kanuri

Homeland: Nigeria, Niger
Religion: Islam

His courtly robes flowing, the dignified
Kanuri official carries the air of his powerful
ancestors. At the height of their empire in
the 16th century, the Kanuri controlled a rich
caravan trade across the Sahara desert. Although no longer controlling great wealth,
the royal and aristocratic classes are still
highly respected in Kanuri society. Deep
scars line the official's face in the distinctive
patterns of his tribe. He has carried these
scars all his life; they were made during a
naming-ceremony when he was just eight
days old, while the *mullah* (religious leader)
read from the Koran. Rituals like the naming
ceremony punctuate and order life in a
Kanuri town. Birth, naming, marriage, death,
and burial all have their ceremonies. Traditional and Islamic holidays mark off the year
and give life meaning and structure.

*Father, we are amazed by the thousands of
rich cultures ordained by your hand. May
Kanuri culture be redeemed for your glory!*

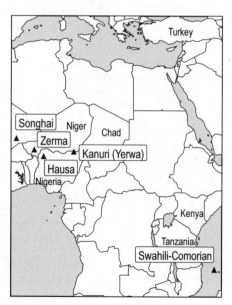

Photo Courtesy Mike Staub, Pioneers.

Jews

The 15 million Jews in the world comprise less than one percent of the earth's population, yet are one the world's most influential people groups. Jewish communities exist in every nation of the Western Hemisphere, most, if not all of the European nations, most of the Middle Eastern and Asian nations, a number of the African nations, Australia, and New Zealand.

Jewish communities are known for strong families, success in business, and emphasis on education and learning. These communities are tied together through national and international organisations. Almost all are spiritually, emotionally, and financially connected to the nation of Israel.

Although both the Old and New Testaments speak of the Jews as God's covenant people, few Jews know why. In spite of their role in God's plan to redeem all nations, few Jews know Jesus as Messiah. In Romans 11:11, Paul says "salvation has come to the Gentiles to make Israel envious." Instead of living a gospel the Jews desire to share, the church has often persecuted the Jews. The 1800 years of Christian anti-Semitism are indeed tragic.

Some of the early church fathers declared Jews cursed forever. Tens of thousands of Jews perished in the Crusades. The Spanish Inquisition killed or exiled 200,000. The Russian and Polish pogroms killed hundreds of thousands more. Through all these and the great tragedy of the Holocaust, the predominantly gentile Christian church has done little to make the Jews envious of the gospel. The weight of world history stands as a great obstacle to the salvation of the world's Jews.

Brothers, my heart's desire and prayer to God for the Israelites is that they may be saved. Romans 10:1

- Come before God in repentance for the church's treatment of Jewish people, and ask him to call more to this ministry of reconciliation.

- More than 30 Messianic Jewish congregations exist in Israel, with more in the US, England, Latin America, and elsewhere. Pray for their growth near and far.

- Pray for the veil to be lifted from the eyes of many more Jews, so that they might see Jesus as the Messiah promised by Moses and the other prophets.

- Spread across the continents, Jews speak many languages and live in many cultures. Some are very religious, others quite secular, yet they see themselves as having a common identity. Ask God to help Jews who follow Jesus to reach other Jews.

Albanians

Homeland: Albania, Yugoslavia
Religion: Islam, Atheism

Today Ramiz will go to church for the very first time. He wonders what to expect. Most Albanians are historically Muslim, and a few are Eastern Orthodox or Catholic. For many years they lived under an atheistic regime. All churches and mosques were closed, their buildings used as warehouses and gymnasiums. Most religious leaders were imprisoned, and Albanians were encouraged to attend secular festivals which the government created. Now that religion is no longer prohibited, religious interest is growing. Most of the remaining clerics, now released from prison, are elderly men.

God, we thank you for Albania's new freedom, and pray that you would raise up strong vibrant Albanian congregations.

Caucasians

Homeland: Russia, Eastern Europe, Central Asia
Religion: Islam

Although Christianity came to the Caucasus mountains centuries ago, most Caucasians are cut off from the gospel today. Almost 40 different languages and many more dialects are spoken in the northern Caucasus region, some of them unwritten, and most unrelated to any other living language. Broken terrain and steep hills isolate Caucasian communities and make travel treacherous. Some communities live as they have for centuries, their lives untouched by the outside world. In other places large Soviet-built cities dominate the landscape and television and radio bring modern values. The many Caucasian languages and dialects have few Bible translations.

Lord, we pray your word would be translated and touch the hearts of the remote peoples of the Caucasus.

Bosnians

Homeland: Bosnia-Hercegovina, Croatia, Montenegro
Religion: Islam

Bosnia is a land of beautiful forests while Hercegovina is majestic with mountains of grey limestone. Together they form the fragile country of Bosnia-Hercegovinia. Formerly part of Yugoslavia, this region is torn by wars rooted in the ethnicity of the Muslim, Catholic and Orthodox peoples. Though many Bosnians are only nominally religious, they claim the religion of their birth, Islam. Several million are now refugees in neighbouring countries.

Prince of Peace, let these war torn peoples find the true and lasting peace that relationship with you can provide.

Siberians

Homeland: Russia
Religion: Shamanism

In forests, mountains and icy tundra live the indigenous peoples of Siberia—more than a million people in some 20 different ethnic groups. Most follow a set of practices collectively known as Shamanism. The word shaman means "he who knows" in the Siberian Tungus language. A shaman is a religious leader skilled in direct communication with spirit powers. Spirits take possession of the shamans, often during a drug-induced trance, and give them powers they use for the well-being of the community, including control of the weather, healing the sick, and guiding the souls of the dead to the spirit world. Many Siberians suffer from depression, emotional problems, and alcoholism because of their fear of the spirit world.

Jesus, let your perfect love meet these Siberian peoples at their greatest need.

People Groups with No Known Christians or Missionaries Working with Them.

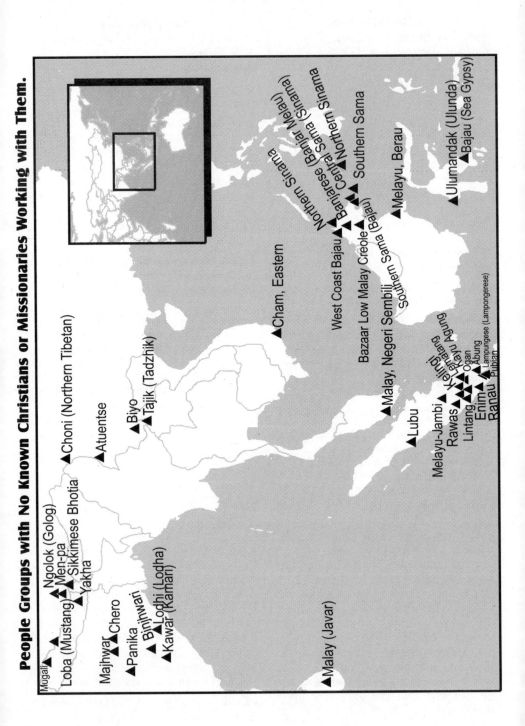

Part III

What's Next?

Just as constantly running water can cut a channel through the hardest rock, so persistent prayer on behalf of unreached peoples has the potential to create channels of God's blessing, resulting in the advance of the gospel. Hopefully, your experience praying for the 10/40 Window will result in continuing prayer and labour for the unreached. Below are a number of ways you can help your church or group continue to be involved.

1. Give a Report to Your Church or Group. A concise and envisioning statement of what occurred while your church or group was praying through the 10/40 Window is a great way to capitalise on the momentum that was generated. This report might be a short announcement, a group testimony, or even a fellowship dinner. Try to find ways to share experiences, impressions, and feelings. Be creative! Be prepared to help others know how they can help.

2. Ongoing Intercession. Consider how your church or group might engage in ongoing intercession. Host a monthly or weekly prayer time and invite others to pray for the unreached. Invite people from other churches to take part. To be effective, each meeting will require planning and preparation. Does someone from your team have interest in facilitating the group? A facilitator can gather prayer letters and news updates from the region to be fuel for prayer and help to lead each meeting.

3. Host a "Sunday for the World." Help your church catch a big-picture vision with an all-church program. This might also be an opportunity to kick off adult-education classes based on *START, Catch the Vision,* or *Destination 2000.* (See the resource list for complete information on these resources.) Any of these Bible-based courses could spring-board your congregation into deeper understanding of and commitment to missions. Consider using drama, video, or some kind of visual demonstration to help capture people's attention and understand missions concepts.

4. Get Involved With the Internet Missions Community. Today the Internet is becoming available in many parts of the world, and Christians are not missing the opportunity. Especially for missions, where one of the major problems is distance and communication, electronic mail or e-mail has become invaluable. What that means for you is that you have the opportunity to be involved in the cutting edge of missions from your school or even your own living room if you have a computer. You can help encourage a missionary by receiving prayer requests from him or her and by helping them find information they need. You can listen in on electronic conferences where the future of missions is being planned today. You can even volunteer to do vital people-group advocacy work by e-mail. See the list of Internet resources at the end of this book for more details.

5. Start Fun Missions Education for Children. A number of excellent and enjoyable Sunday school programs for children are available which help draw kids into the action. Included are Bible stories which show how God's heart is for all nations, activities to teach kids how to pray for unreached people groups and the missionaries working with them, and other motivating lessons. Check with the organisations listed at the end of this book to find what is available in your area.

6. Host a Concert of Prayer. Invite people from many different churches to come together for one evening for a Concert of Prayer. Divide the evening into short "seasons" of prayer, with each season having a slightly different prayer focus. Each season should begin with an explanation of the prayer focus and how to pray for that topic. It is helpful to sing and worship between seasons as well.

7. Send a Prayer Journey Team. Many from your church may show interest in visiting the peoples for whom they have prayed. Prayer Journeys are great ways to help your church or group gain face-to-face experience with the unreached and begin to plan how to be involved long-term. Praying on-site not only produces more informed prayer, but also produces strategic relationships with Christian workers on the field. These relationships are one of the best ways for your church or group to invest itself strategically.

8. Church-Leadership Expeditions. Consider planning a special *leadership expedition* from your church to follow-up the efforts of the initial prayer effort. These follow-up trips would help your leaders to be able to influence your whole fellowship as they discover firsthand insights about these relatively unknown peoples.

A church-leadership expedition is similar to but distinct from a prayer journey. For example, it might have a shorter time frame. It should incorporate many of the same aspects as a prayer journey: on-site intercession, briefings and interaction with indigenous pastors and expatriate workers, and face-to-face encounters with unreached peoples. It should, however, devote more time to discussing and praying about specific roles your group can play in long-term ministry there.

9. Develop Your Group's World Christian Leadership. Encourage a few key people from your leadership team to attend a conference or gathering of missions activists. In the US, *Advancing Church Missions Commitment (ACMC)* conferences are good for this purpose. There are many organisations in the final section of this book which can refer you to a conference near you. You may also find classes available at a local college or university which can help develop missions leaders within your group. Ask if the excellent *Perspectives on the World Christian Movement* course is available near you.

10. Adopting Unreached Peoples. Encourage your church to consider "adopting" one specific unreached people for long-term ministry. To be effective, your whole church should embrace the adoption and integrate it into the life of the fellowship. For more information on what it means to "adopt" an unreached people group, contact one of the agencies listed in the appendix.

11. International Student Ministry. There are over 400,000 international students studying in universities, junior and community colleges, and language centres throughout the United States with many others in all the major European cities. In many cases, they represent the very peoples and cities for which you have been praying. Their presence is one way that God has brought the nations right to our doorstep. One creative step that you might take is to minister to international students in your own community. Although there are a number of ministries focused on international students, the largest in the US is International Students Incorporated.

12. Prayerwalking Right at Home. Praying for unreached peoples can lead to a heightened concern for needs in your own city. It is quite natural that your church would incorporate prayerwalking into a strategy of reaching your community. Consider leading prayerwalking workshops for your church. Some who thought they would never go overseas on a prayer journey may change their minds after they prayerwalk through their own neighbourhoods.

13. Adopting a Missionary or a Project. Though most unreached peoples have very little Christian activity focused on them, many of them do have small works or projects which are just beginning. These start-up teams or projects are always under-funded and under-supported. If your church or group can find one of these teams or projects, it is a tremendous encouragement to those involved for you to seek them out and offer your assistance. Single out one of these people or projects to focus on with prayer, finances, and other assistance. A church's committed and faithful backing means a great deal to those labouring in spiritually isolated situations, and every missionary can be more effective with more finances, prayer, and people backing him or her.

14. Send a "Missionary" from Your Church. Through the course of the prayer project, many in your church will learn about a number of people groups, perhaps for the first time. This is a key time to be inviting or challenging people throughout your church to become "missionaries." Many agencies list their greatest need to be teachers or administrative helpers. Make sure people know that one does not have to have seminary training to be effectively used on the field. Try to offer opportunities for all kinds of people, young or old, experts or beginners. Encourage some to think about getting the training required to become church planters, but ensure that everyone in the congregation knows there are overseas service opportunities for them, perhaps in teaching English or in a critical support role.

If someone from your church shows interest in full-time cross-cultural ministry, be quick to rally support for them from the church. Encourage everyone in your congregation or group that Jesus can take our five loaves and two fish and use them to feed a multitude. Help anyone who shows interest to quickly get in contact with mission agencies or others who can help them get to the field.

15. Championing the Vision. Because of the growing prayer movement for the unreached peoples in the 10/40 Window, a number of churches may be sending prayer teams to the same cities and people groups. Vision is growing throughout the church for completing world evangelisation; soon there will be networks of churches, organisations, and individual Christians committed to seeing churches planted among every unevangelised people group. Perhaps you or someone you know can become a champion for one specific people group, networking and co-operating with others who focus on the same group. You can be a point-person for your church, finding ways your fellowship can co-operate with other churches, advocating for your specific unreached people. If you would like more information on how to "advocate" for a specific unreached people group, contact Caleb Project – People Specific Advocates.

16. Send a Church-Planting Team. Perhaps your church or group has the unique gifts required to actually send a church-planting team to minister among an unreached people group. This is not at all an easy task. Some churches have found great success forming a partnership with a missions agency that has experience in sending church-planting teams. Sending a church-planting team is a serious commitment, but one with great rewards.

People-Group Advocacy

A new role in missions has come to light in the last ten years. These missionaries rarely share their faith, publish literature, or preach in a foreign language. Some never even meet a person from the ethnic group their ministry emphasises. Yet without their catalytic influence, the work among these unreached people groups might never begin.

These missionaries are *people-group advocates*. An advocate is one who pleads another's case (a lawyer) or a person who speaks or writes in support of something. Advocates adopt another's needs for fluent representation in a realm inaccessible to the other. Each people-group advocate helps bridge the gap between a specific unreached people group (realm 1) and specific resources within the kingdom of God (realm 2). Kingdom resources might be local churches, missions agencies, individuals, emergency aid organisations, community development teams, financial donors, prayer warriors, Bible and literature translators and producers, church planters, or even ministry support services like schools for missionary kids. Unfortunately, these two realms are completely inaccessible to one another except by those God raises up to bridge this gap.

Why Advocate?

Most unreached people groups live in difficult circumstances geographically, politically, and socially. It is, therefore, all the more essential that ministry in these circumstances is fine-tuned for the situation. The advocacy ministry has grown out of this reality.

Because Advocates Bring People Groups into Focus

Unreached peoples need advocates within the kingdom learning about them, praying for them specifically, and calling for co-operation in loving and strategic initiative. For the church, "out of sight" usually means "out of mind." Advocates bring the unreached peoples clearly into our vision.

Have we taken steps to assure we are working in co-operation? Have we assigned project-hours to cultural understanding, partnership, and co-operation? Advocacy builds people-group oriented relationships that form the infrastructure for culturally enlightened co-operation.

Because Each People Group Is a Treasure

Each people group is like a field with a treasure buried in it. That treasure is God's unique plan of salvation for that people. It is the joy of advocacy to become fully invested in one of God's nations and then to behold the "Day of Mercy" for that people – perhaps only by faith. Few, however, are willing to buy the field.

No Such Thing As a Closed Country

No people group is inaccessible today. Advocates can help find access for long-term and short-term workers. Those working in these "creative-access areas" are often quite restricted both on and off the field. However, because advocates may work entirely outside of restricted areas, they can often operate very publicly and with few restrictions. As a trusted "front" for workers in the field, an advocate can support the field operations effectively.

Furthermore, missionaries from the developing world can enter where others cannot. In these situations advocates are critical for building bridges of co-operation, benefiting these workers and the wider missions community.

Learning, Linking, and Loving

Advocates **learn** about two areas: (1) about the people group, their culture, environment, and current status, and (2) about the kingdom resources: who is working with or who could work with the people group. Each advocate will develop a unique network among kingdom resources. Then advocates **link** the right resources with the right opportunities.

Advocates seek God to build **love** in their hearts for the people group. One of the best ways to begin is regular prayer for the unreached people group. As an advocate prays and encourages others to pray, God builds compassion.

More than anything today we need advocates who can seek out others with potential interest in their chosen people and help them into ministry. We need individuals who will work together as a team, building relationships of trust and partnership with people from other churches, denominations, traditions, approaches, and countries. People-group advocates must reach across the barriers which have kept the unreached peoples unreached.

Communication: An Advocate's Tool to Build a Network

Advocates invest much of their time in communication: sharing information about their chosen people group, needs or opportunities for ministry, or more personally, expressing a God-given passion for their chosen people. Because of this, letters, the phone, fax, and especially electronic mail (e-mail) are all of great value to an advocate.

An Advocate's Commitment

Commitment to an unreached people group is the defining element of advocacy. Without this commitment there can be no advocate. God often uses the advocate's commitment to draw others into ministry among the advocate's chosen people group. Advocates commit to build bridge-relationships for co-operative ministry based on a healthy understanding of the people group.

Danger: Prayer Journey Coming

A Brief Look at Prayer Journey Precautions

What better way to learn about the unreached than to visit an unreached people group, see what their lives are like and, through on-site prayer, seek God's will for them? This is the agenda of a prayer-journey team, a small group of people, usually sent by their church to an unreached people group in which they have a particular interest. Prayer journeys always involve prayer walking: praying with your eyes open as you walk down the very streets where you expect to see God answer your prayers. It's a dynamic combination—*praying* for the things you see and *seeing* with the hope and perspective that come from prayer.

In October 1995, thousands of Christians took prayer journeys to visit the 100 "Gateway Cities" of the 10/40 Window. While we hope *Praying through the Window III* will mobilise even more prayer-journey teams, we must offer a few words of caution. Prayer journeys are dangerous. They take on spiritual battles and threaten Satan's strongholds. But the danger is not just for the demons. Prayer journeys can put team members, local Christians, and long-term workers in danger as well.

Honour Your Hosts

A prayer journey is an excellent way to serve members of the missionary community by coming alongside them, learning about and joining in the battles they fight every day. Indeed, most prayer-journey teams visit missionaries their churches support. But, like other short-term mission projects, prayer-journey teams sometimes hurt the long-term workers more than they help them. If you are arrogant, brash, or independent, you will be a liability to your hosts. The keys to being a blessing are humility, respect, and listening. Long-term workers have invested much more in serving the people group than you have. God has sent you for a purpose, and the things he does through your team may provide instruction or example for the long-term workers, but more likely it will be the other way around. Listen to them. Respect them. Honour God by honouring your hosts. Try to give back to them twice as much as they sacrifice for you.

Exercise special caution in the area of evangelism. Giving a Bible to your translator or cook may be perfectly acceptable, but performing an evangelistic drama in the park next to your hotel may not be acceptable. If possible, ask what is acceptable and under what circumstances. What you do reflects on those who invited you, those who associate with you, those who arranged your visas, and even those who resemble you.

Show Respect for Local Authorities

Be cautious about going where you are not invited. If you are in a Muslim city, for instance, visiting a mosque may be a powerful and valuable experience for you, but taking photographs may or may not be an acceptable way to steward this experience! Present your request to someone who has the authority to make this decision, and be patient with local bureaucracy or relationships. You may not have to face the consequences of breaking the rules; your hosts might face these consequences instead.

Trust God If Trouble Comes

Recognise that some things may happen that are beyond your control. Being arrested or detained by the police, for example, does not necessarily mean you have done something wrong. You may be stopped unexpectedly in places where foreigners seldom go or where bribery is common. Be patient and trust the Lord to help you. There may also be local political situations of which you are unaware. A short-term team in Turkey was deported the morning after they unknowingly accepted an invitation to visit a Turkish family who turned out to be leaders in an opposition political party. As you go, ask God to protect you. Encourage those who are staying home to pray for you.

Avoid Distractions

Some of the challenges you face may be purely practical. Recognise that in many of the areas where unreached people live, a group of foreigners may be a fascinating oddity. One man, pale, blond, and well over six feet tall, drew a great deal of attention as he tried to quietly prayer-walk in a Southeast Asian city. As his team walked through quiet streets, people would call out to them, eager to practice their English or entertain an American guest. Be polite, but try to keep your focus on what you've come to do. Just as the nationals may be curious about you, your team will surely be curious about them. The desire to take photos or shop for souvenirs is natural. Set aside a separate time for these activities. Don't let them distract you from your purpose.

Be practical

Don't be afraid to spend enough money on conveniences like hiring someone to cook for you. If you have limited time in an area, make the most of it by renting a van or using taxis instead of struggling to learn the local transportation system. Your journey will also be easier if you bring clothing that is comfortable, modest, and inconspicuous.

Long prayer walks, especially in the hot sun, can be very draining. Some teams make the mistake of thinking that being spiritual means they must walk until they cannot take another step. By burning out and using up team members, you lose the long-term impact you could have by sending team members home with excitement, vision, and love for the people they have met.

Look for Reasons to Hope

Some prayer journey leaders make the mistake of only taking their teams to the dark places: the slums, garbage dumps, mosques, and temples. Balance these visits by spending time with bright, hopeful Christian workers or local believers, so team members can return home with hope and vision for their host people. Give them a chance to fall in love with the city and its people. God is working among the unreached peoples of the world. Don't miss your chance to see it firsthand!

What is the Joshua Project 2000 list?

The list is a way to look at information about peoples currently without an adequate indigenous network of churches. These peoples either have no church of their own or have a Christian community so small that it cannot yet reach the extremities of their own people. The information in the list should help the global church work and pray toward the establishment of churches in each of these "least-evangelised" peoples in the remaining years of this millennium.

How was it compiled?

A small international team compiled hundreds of pieces of data from several databases of the world's peoples. With the input of church and mission leaders worldwide, they sought to determine which peoples are the world's least-evangelised.

The team made a difficult, but necessary, decision to limit the list based on two important selection criteria:

First, the list is limited primarily to peoples with populations of 10,000 or more. The list's editorial committee noted that many of the least-evangelised peoples with small populations may be grouped with their larger parent body, even though they may be geographically separated from them.

Second, the list is limited to peoples with an Evangelical Protestant community less than 2% or a total Christian community less than 5% of the overall population. In a few cases, exceptions were made. Peoples with larger Protestant or Christian communities were included on the list because the committee felt these peoples warrant new or continuing ministry efforts in the months and years between now and the turn of the century.

Are these peoples more important than other peoples who are not on the list?

No. All the unreached peoples need a culturally relevant church. Larger, more comprehensive lists of all peoples do exist. This list is intended to be a helpful tool for the global church as we seek to work together to see a church planted in every people by the year 2000. The Joshua Project 2000 list is the first attempt to clearly identify the least evangelised peoples of the world. The list exists so that the church worldwide may focus her work and prayers where they are most needed and where they may be most effective right now, at the close of the 20th century.

The list is being continually evaluated and will be annually revised to correct inconsistencies and errors and to reflect updated information. Suggested revisions may be made to John Gilbert, 3806 Monument Ave., Richmond, VA 23230 USA, E-mail: 753-8054@MCIMAIL.COM, Fax: (804) 254-8980.

What information does the list contain?

The complete list contains 17 pieces of data for each of the 1746 peoples in it. The shorter list in this book contains only six pieces of information for each of the peoples.

Affinity Bloc: A broad grouping of all the peoples by language, culture, religion, and politics. Every bloc may contain widely dissimilar and unrelated linguistic minorities, but often there is one particular culture that is dominant.

Gateway People Cluster (GPC): Closely related peoples within each bloc clustered together, based on a common identity of language or name, or on culture, religion, economy. Most peoples in the list may be grouped in Gateway People clusters of which almost all have total populations of over one million. In many cases the Gateway People Name represents one of the peoples in that cluster which is a strategic "gateway" for purposes of evangelism for the cluster.

People name: The name of the specific ethno-linguistic people within that cluster and affinity bloc. Alternative names appear in parentheses behind the primary people name.

Country name: The country in which this people lives. Some people may live in more than one country. This list contains every country in which 10,000 or more of these people live.

Population: The population of this people within this country, in thousands.

Priority ranking: The larger, more comprehensive Joshua Project 2000 list ranks the peoples according to ministry need. The scale ranges from 1 (highest priority) to 9 (lowest priority). The ranking was based on a weighted factoring of five items: Percent Evangelical (weighted at 30%), Church Status (25%), available Ministry Tools like Bible translations and radio programming (20%), Agency Work among them (15%), and Population (10%).

For example, a group with no known evangelicals, no known churches, no ministry tools, no agency work and a large population would receive a priority of 1. This is admittedly an imperfect system as the unknown data tends to skew a ranking toward a higher priority than may be actually true. Our list indicates the peoples ranked 1 or 2 by underlining their country and population numbers.

Remember, the list is a tool to fuel your prayers and church-planting efforts. Our prayer is that you'll join millions of Christians around the globe to use it often and well!

List of Joshua-Project 2000 Peoples

Arab World

Arabian Arab
Arab: Pakistan 142k, India 95k, Bosnia-Hercegovina 32k, Philippines 21k, Malaysia 10k
Bahraini Arab: Bahrain 528k
Coast Arab: Tanzania 235k, Kenya 73k
Hijazi-Arab: Saudi Arabia 11,590k
Iranian Arab: Iran 600k
Iraqi Arab: Kuwait 131k
Mahra: Oman 109k
Mahra (Mehri, Mahri): Yemen 294k
Mahra (South Arabic): Saudi Arabia 17k
Omani Arab: Oman 900k, United Arab Emirates 193k, Yemen 98k, Saudi Arabia 68k, Djibouti 57k, Somalia 33k, Kuwait 12k
Saudi Arab: Saudi Arabia 2,000k, United Arab Emirates 400k, Oman 50k
Shahara: Saudi Arabia 34k
Socotra (Sokotri): Yemen 59k
Zott Gypsy (Nawar): Iran 80k, Iraq 50k, United Arab Emirates 12k

Bedouin - Arabian
Bedouin: Egypt 1,100k
Bedouin Arab: Saudi Arabia 3,000k, Jordan 1,000k, Syria 1,000k, Israel 732k
Gulf Bedouin: United Arab Emirates 167k

Bedouin - Saharan
Bedouin Arab: Burkina Faso 10k
Chaamba Bedouin: Algeria 60k
Fezzan Bedouin: Libya 168k
Gafsa Bedouin: Tunisia 30k
Kufra Bedouin: Libya 22k
Kunta Bedouin: Mali 106k
Riyah Bedouin: Libya 28k
Saharan Arab: Mali 106k
Sahel Bedouin: Tunisia 1,900k
Sanusi Bedouin: Libya 505k
Sirtican Bedouin: Libya 28k

Egyptian
Arab: Bangladesh 39k
Arabized Nubian: Egypt 292k
Egyptian Arab: Egypt 44,500k

Hassaniya
Arab: Senegal 10k
Berabish Bedouin: Mali 106k
Black Moor (Maure): Senegal 10k
Hassaniya speakers: Morocco
Maure (Moor): Gambia 15k
Moor (Maure): Niger 127k

Moor (Maure, Bidan): Mali 106k
Moor (White): Morocco 20k
Saharawi: Morocco
White Moor (Bidan): Senegal 10k

Kabyle Berber
Kabyle: Algeria 2,000k, Belgium 49k

Levant Arab
Arab: Iraq 4,000k
Iraqi Arab: Syria 75k
Iraqi Kurd: Iraq 1,457k
Jordanian Arab: Syria 10,000k, Saudi Arabia 86k
Palestinian Arab: Jordan 3,160k, Lebanon 364k, Egypt 117k, Libya 54k, Iraq 34k, Yemen 14k
Syrian Arab: Kuwait 10k

Libyan Arab
Arabized Black: Libya 98k
Cyernaican Arab: Libya 1,400k
Jalo Berber: Libya
Tripolitanian Arab: Libya 229k

Maghreb Arab
Algerian Arab: France 800k, Tunisia 218k, Morocco 198k, Belgium 15k
Algerian Arab (Jazair): Algeria 19,865k
Arabized Berber: Egypt 1,167k, Libya 228k, France 114k, Belgium 39k, Netherlands 23k
Maghrib Arab: Sudan 139k
Moroccan Arab: Morocco 16,000k, France 700k, Belgium 130k, Netherlands 100k, Germany 25k
North African Arab: Italy 22k
Tunisian Arab: Tunisia 7,300k, France 250k, Libya 159k

Other
Chaldean: Iraq 160k
Jebala: Morocco
Nefusa Berber: Libya 40k
Samaritan (Shomronim): Israel 128k
Zuara (Zwara, Zuraa): Libya 33k

Riff Berber
Ghomara Berber: Morocco 57k
Northern Shilha: Morocco 1,273k, Algeria 255k
Riffian: France 57k

Saharan Berber
Gadames Berber: Libya 25k
Ghardaia Berber: Algeria 80k
Gourara Berber: Algeria 20k
Siwa (Oasis Berber): Egypt 30k
Tidikelt Berber: Algeria 14k
Tit Berber: Algeria 14k
Tougourt Berber: Algeria 57k

Tuat Berber: Algeria 57k
Wargla Berber (Ouargla): Algeria 57k
Zenaga (Berber): Mauritania 16k

Shawiya Berber
Shawiya: France 114k
Shawiya (Chaouia): Algeria 1,700k

Shilha Berber
Drawa Berber: Morocco 3,000k
Southern Shilha: Morocco 3,000k, Algeria 230k

Shuwa Arab
Fertit (Baggara): Central African Republic 65k
Habbania (Baggara): Sudan 215k
Selim (Baggara): Sudan 38k
Shuwa Arab (Baggara): Chad 1,560k, Nigeria 100k, Cameroon 64k, Niger 50k
Shuwa Arab (Chad Arab): Central African Republic 11k

Sudan Arab
Amri: Sudan 47k
Arabized Burun: Sudan 18k
Arabized Ghulfan: Sudan 16k
Arabized Karko: Sudan 13k
Arabized Mararit: Sudan 20k
Arabized Midob (Tidda): Sudan 30k
Arabized Nyimang: Sudan 70k
Arabized Tagale: Sudan 36k
Arabized Temein: Sudan 10k
Arabized Tira: Sudan 40k
Awlad Hassan: Sudan 58k
Batahin: Sudan 155k
Bederia: Sudan 581k
Dar Hamid: Sudan 465k
Dubasiyin: Sudan 65k
Fezara: Sudan 203k
Gaaliin: Sudan 1,950k
Gawamaa: Sudan 601k
Gimma: Sudan 99k
Guhayna: Sudan 904k
Hamar: Sudan 262k
Hasania: Sudan 458k
Hawawir: Sudan 150k
Husseinat: Sudan 99k
Juba Somali: Ethiopia 267k, Somalia 253k
Kababish: Sudan 241k
Kawahla (Fezara): Sudan 599k
Kerarish: Sudan 27k
Lahawin: Sudan 98k
Liri: Sudan 38k
Maalia: Sudan 69k
Messiria (Baggara): Sudan
Mongallese Arab: Sudan 20k
Rashaida: Sudan 68k

Rizeiqat (Habbania): Sudan 248k
Rufaa (Rufaiyin): Sudan 356k
Shaikia: Sudan 613k
Sherifi: Sudan 112k
Shukria: Sudan 164k
Sudanese Arab: Sudan 15,000k,
Egypt 1,000k, Yemen 238k,
Libya 191k, Ethiopia 107k,
Saudi Arabia 86k, United Arab
Emirates 18k
Tungur: Sudan 163k
Turku Arab (Tekrur): Chad 13k
Yazeed: Sudan

Tamazight
Beraber: France 114k
Central Shilha: Morocco 1,900k, Al-
geria 60k
Nail Bedouin: Algeria 28k

Tuareg
Ahaggaren: Algeria 31k
Air Tuareg (Air): Niger 250k
Tahoua Tuareg: Niger 350k, Mali
190k
Tamasheq, Timbuktu: Mali 250k
Tuareg (Aulliminden): Nigeria 23k
Tuareg (Udalan): Burkina Faso 50k
Udalan Tuareg: Mali 259k

Yemeni Arab
Arabized Black: Yemen 154k
Yemeni Arab: Yemen 12,560k,
Saudi Arabia 120k, Egypt
116k, Djibouti 46k, Madagas-
car 28k, Sudan 15k, United
Arab Emirates 15k, Somalia
10k, Ethiopia 10k

Horn of Africa; Cushitic Peoples

Afar
Danakil (Afar): Somalia 488k, Dji-
bouti 200k
Danakil (Afar, Adali): Ethiopia 450k

Beja
Beja, Beni-Amer: Sudan 1,907k,
Ethiopia 39k
Bisharin (Ababdah): Egypt 58k

Other
Ajuran: Kenya 64k
Garreh: Kenya 64k
Gawwada (Gauwada): Ethiopia 50k
Guarage, Silti: Ethiopia 493k
Hamer-Banna: Ethiopia 20k
Harari (Adere): Ethiopia 16k
Libido (Maraqo): Ethiopia 100k
Orma (Orma Galla): Kenya 40k
Raya Galla (Azebu): Ethiopia 54k
Reshiat (Dasenech): Ethiopia 34k
Saho: Ethiopia 120k
Tigre: Ethiopia 54k, Sudan 12k
Zayse: Ethiopia 20k

Somali
Gosha: Somalia 168k, Kenya 17k
Somali: Somalia 7,500k, Ethiopia
888k, Kenya 362k, Yemen

230k, Saudi Arabia 34k, Tanza-
nia 33k
Somali (Issa): Djibouti 181k, United
Arab Emirates 25k

Sub-Saharan African

Chad-Saharan
Arabized Zaghawa: Sudan 102k
Awlad Mana: Sudan 102k
Bideyat (Beri): Chad 47k
Daza (Dazaga): Niger 182k
Daza (Dazagada): Chad 282k
Kanembu: Chad 67k
Teda (Tubu): Niger 40k, Libya 16k
Teda (Tubu, Gorane): Chad 29k
Zaghawa: Sudan 102k, Niger 35k
Zaghawa (Zeghawa): Chad 18k

Chadic - Nigeria, Chad, & Sudan
Afade: Cameroon 14k
Bade: Nigeria 250k
Baldamu (Mbazia): Cameroon 14k
Banana: Chad 100k
Bidio; Bidiyo: Chad 14k
Buduma (Kuri Islander): Chad 25k
Buta-Ningi (Butawa): Nigeria 27k
Daffo-Batura (Chala): Nigeria 13k
Dangaleat: Chad 17k
Duwai: Nigeria 13k
Fali (Bana): Nigeria 96k, Cameroon
13k
Galambi (Galambawa): Nigeria 20k
Gera (Gerawa): Nigeria 13k
Goemai (Ankwe): Nigeria 568k
Gude (Cheke, Mubi): Cameroon 28k
Guduf (Gudupe, Gvoko): Nigeria 21k
Gulfe (Gulfei, Malgwe): Cameroon
56k
Guruntum (Guruntawa): Nigeria 15k
Gwandara: Nigeria 30k
Jongor (Dionkor, Djonkor): Chad
14k
Kajakse: Chad 10k
Kotoko (Moria, Bara): Cameroon
31k
Kotoko-Logone: Chad 13k
Kulung: Chad 100k
Laamang (Xedi, Hide): Cameroon
14k
Mada: Cameroon 17k
Mandara (Wandala): Cameroon
24k, Nigeria 20k
Mefele: Cameroon 10k
Mousgoum (Moului): Chad 75k
Muyang (Myau): Cameroon 15k
Ngossi (Gevoko): Cameroon 52k
North Mofu: Cameroon 56k
Podoko, Podokwo, Pare: Cameroon
30k
Warji (Warjawa): Nigeria 70k
Wuzlam (Uzam): Cameroon 11k
Zulgo (Zelgwa, Mineo): Cameroon
18k

Dioula
Bobo Jula (Zara): Burkina Faso 200k
Dyula (Jula, Wangara): Ghana 18k

Dyula, Djoula, Malink: Cote d'Ivoire
1,470k
Jula (Dyula): Burkina Faso 1,000k
Jula (Dyula, Kong Jula): Mali 50k
Wala (Dagaari Jula): Burkina Faso
36k

Fula
Adamawa Fulani, Puel: Cameroon
669k
Bagirmi Fula: Chad 24k
Bagirmi Fulani: Central African Re-
public 108k
Bauchi Fulani: Nigeria 2,171k
Benin-Togo Fulani: Togo 37k
Bororo Fulani (Mbororro):
Cameroon 112k
Fula (Fulani), Peulh: Benin 224k
Fula (Macina, Liptako): Burkina
Faso 354k
Fula Jalon (Futa Dyalon): Guinea
2,550k
Fula Jalon (Futa Jallon): Sierra
Leone 178k
Fula Kita (Peuhala): Mali 911k
Fula Macina: Mali 116k
Fula Toro (Fula Jeeri): Senegal 350k
Fulakunda (Fula Cunda): Senegal
1,455k, Guinea-Bissau 180k
Fulani: Chad 758k
Fulani (Fulakunda): Gambia 168k
Fulani (Sudanese Fula): Sudan 130k
Futa Jalon (Futa Fula): Senegal 100k
Gurma Fulani (Fulbe): Burkina Faso
624k
Krio Fula: Sierra Leone 48k
Sokoto Fulani: Nigeria 1,921k, Ni-
ger 710k
Tukulor (Haalpulaaren): Mauritania
150k
Tukulor (Takarir): Senegal 662k,
Mali 135k, Gambia 59k
Western Fulani (Bororo): Niger 182k

Gur
Bassari (Basari, Ncham): Ghana 100k
Birifor: Ghana 63k
Bondoukou Kulango: Ghana 10k
Burba (Berba, Biali): Benin 65k
Chamba (Kasele): Togo 34k
Diamala Senufo: Cote d'Ivoire 12k
Ditamari: Benin 136k
Doghosie (Dorosie): Burkina Faso
20k
Dompago (Lokpa): Togo 125k
Gangam (Ngangan, Dye): Togo 34k
Gurma: Togo 121k
Jaan (Yana): Burkina Faso 16k
Kolsi (Ko, Kols): Burkina Faso 16k
Kotokoli (Tem): Benin 42k
Kotokoli (Tem, Temba): Ghana 65k
Kotokoli (Tim, Temba): Togo 204k
Kulango, Bouna: Ghana 16k
Kulele (Coulailai): Cote d'Ivoire 24k
Lamba (Namba, Losso): Togo 117k
Lobi (Lobiri): Burkina Faso 286k,
Cote d'Ivoire 156k
Mamara Senufo: Mali 500k

Mbelime (Niendi): Benin 31k
Nanerge Senufo: Burkina Faso 106k
Nanumba (Nunuma): Ghana 36k
Natemba: Benin 54k
Puguli (Pwa): Burkina Faso 13k
Senoufo, Niarafolo-Niafolo: Cote
  d'Ivoire 13k
Somba (Tamberma): Togo 20k
Southern Sisaala: Ghana 50k
Suppire Senufo: Mali 364k
Tamprusi (Tampele): Ghana 40k
Toussian (Win): Burkina Faso 25k
Turka (Tyurama): Burkina Faso 40k
Tyelibele: Cote d'Ivoire 15k
Waama (Yoabu): Benin 47k, Togo
  11k
Wala (Waali): Ghana 99k
Western Karaboro: Burkina Faso
  30k
Zaore: Burkina Faso 25k

Hausa: Ghana 162k, Chad 100k,
  Cote d'Ivoire 87k, Ethiopia
  54k, Cameroon 24k
Hausa (Hausawa): Nigeria 23,180k
Hausa (Tazarawa): Niger 3,352k
Hausa Fulani: Sudan 90k
Toroobe Fulani: Nigeria 6,250k

Kanuri: Sudan 195k
Manga Kanuri: Niger 500k, Nigeria
  200k
Yerwa Kanuri: Nigeria 4,411k, Chad
  100k, Cameroon 57k, Niger
  50k

Bambara, Falani: Mali 2,969k
Dialonke (Yalunka): Mali 11k
Jahanka (Diakhanke): Senegal 22k
Kagoro (Logoro): Mali 15k
Khasonke (Kasonke): Mali 120k
Konyanke: Cote d'Ivoire 131k,
  Guinea 13k
Koranko: Guinea 55k
Kuranko (Koranko): Sierra Leone
  210k
Malinke: Burkina Faso 83k
Malinke (Malinka): Senegal 259k
Malinke (Mandinka): Guinea-Bissau
  108k
Mandingo (Maninka): Liberia 34k
Mandinka: Senegal 446k
Mandinka (Sose): Gambia 354k
Maninka: Guinea-Bissau 127k,
  Senegal 25k
Maninka (Mandingo): Sierra Leone
  106k
Maninka (South Malinka): Guinea
  1,641k
Manya (Manya Kan): Liberia 45k
Yalunka (Dyalonke): Guinea 147k
Yalunka (Yalun Soso): Sierra Leone
  28k

Dongolawi Nubian: Egypt 759k

Fedicca-Mahas Nubian: Egypt 292k
Ghulfan (Gulfan): Sudan 16k
Kenuzi-Dongolese Nubi: Sudan
  200k
Midob (Meidob, Tiddi): Sudan 30k
Nubian (Sudanese): Uganda 15k,
  Kenya 10k

Aizo: Benin 202k
Aja-Gbe: Togo 111k
Akebou: Togo 41k
Amo: Nigeria 199k
Anuak: Sudan 30k
Anufo: Togo 42k
Atwot: Sudan 25k
Aukwe (Auen): Botswana 11k
Awak: Nigeria 13k
Banda (Ligbi, Weela): Ghana 10k
Bande (Bandi, Gbandi): Guinea 85k
Banga (Bangawa): Nigeria 16k
Bangwinji: Nigeria 12k
Banta: Sierra Leone 14k
Banyun (Banyuk,Elomay): Senegal
  21k
Baraca: Cote d'Ivoire 50k
Baraguyu: Tanzania 689k
Bolon: Burkina Faso 11k
Bozo: Mali 100k
Bubi: Equatorial Guinea 22k
Bukakhwe, Tannekwe: Botswana
  12k
Bullom (Northern Bullom): Sierra
  Leone 38k
Central Dinka: Sudan 29k
Central Koma (Komo): Sudan 10k
Cham-Mwana: Nigeria 13k
Crioulo: Sao Tome and Principe 98k
Didinga (Xaroxa,Toi): Sudan 58k
Digo: Kenya 360k, Tanzania 100k
Diola (Jola, Joola): Guinea-Bissau
  19k
Dirim: Nigeria 11k
Dogon: Mali 425k
Doka: Nigeria 13k
Dong (Donga): Nigeria 13k
Donyiro: Ethiopia 32k
Duguri (Dugurawa): Nigeria 12k
Dukawa (Dukkawa): Nigeria 73k
Duli (Dui): Cameroon 14k
Duun (Samogho, Duu): Mali 70k
Eloyi (Afo): Nigeria 25k
Fang (Okak): Equatorial Guinea
  255k
Foodo: Benin 12k
Gengle: Nigeria 13k
Gio: Liberia 151k
Gola: Liberia 99k
Grebo, Fopo-Bua: Liberia 17k
Gusilay: Senegal 17k
Heikum (San): Namibia 30k
Hwla: Togo 32k
Idon (Idong): Nigeria 13k
Iku: Nigeria 13k
Indo-Mauritian: South Africa 39k
Izere: Nigeria 30k
Jumjum (Wadega): Sudan 25k

Kaba Demi (Deme): Chad 40k
Kaba Na (Tie, Dindjo): Chad 35k
Kalanga: Botswana 120k
Kami: Tanzania 315k
Kara: Central African Republic 13k
Kasa (Casa): Senegal 30k
Kasem (Kasena): Burkina Faso 100k
Katla (Akalak): Sudan 14k
Kissi: Guinea 287k
Koma Ndera: Nigeria 32k
Kono: Cote d'Ivoire 15k
Koro: Nigeria 299k
Krongo Nuba: Sudan 22k
Kulango, Bouna: Cote d'Ivoire 142k
Kunante (Maswanka): Guinea 11k
Kuo: Cameroon 40k
Kupsabiny: Uganda 110k
Kwanka (Kadun): Nigeria 224k
Laka: Chad 40k
Landoma (Landouman): Guinea 14k
Liko: Zaire 60k
Loko (Landogo): Guinea 26k
Lulba: Uganda 15k
Maban-Jumjum (Meban): Sudan 25k
Maca: Mozambique 300k
Madi: Uganda 131k
Mahi: Togo 25k
Makua (Makhua): Comoros 11k
Makua (Makhua, Makoa): Madagas-
  car 152k
Mambwe-Lungu: Tanzania 97k
Mandyak (Manfaco): Guinea 21k
Mandyak (Manjaco): Senegal 70k,
  France 22k, Gambia 17k
Mankanya (Mancanha): Guinea 30k
Mano (Ngere, Mawe): Guinea 34k
Marendje: Mozambique 403k
Marfa: Chad 130k
Mashi Bushman: Zambia 21k
Mau (Mahu): Cote d'Ivoire 169k
Maviha (Mawia): Tanzania 70k
Mesengo (Majang): Ethiopia 28k
Monkole (Mokole): Benin 78k
Morisyen: Mauritania 600k
Mumuye: Cameroon 400k
Murle (Boma): Sudan 60k
Mursi (Murzu): Ethiopia 39k
Mwani (Ibo, Quimuane): Mozam-
  bique 100k
Myene: Gabon 35k
Nara (Barea, Barya): Ethiopia 39k
Ndengereko: Tanzania 110k
Ndut: Senegal 21k
Ngan (Nguin, Gan, Beng): Cote
  d'Ivoire 17k
Ngiti: Zaire 100k
Ngomba: Cameroon 20k
Njeng: Cameroon 29k
North Fali: Cameroon 16k
North Koma (Kwama): Ethiopia 15k
Nyiha (Nyasa Nyika): Zambia 306k
Nyimang (Nyima, Ama): Sudan 70k
Ogori-Magongo: Nigeria 10k
Pari (Lokoro): Sudan 28k
Puku (Faka, Aror): Nigeria 36k
Rufiji (Ruihi, Fiji): Tanzania 200k

Samogho, Dzungo: Burkina Faso 12k
Sehwi: Cote d'Ivoire 150k
Serer-Non: Senegal 21k
Serer-Safen (Safi): Senegal 35k
Shanga (Shangawa): Nigeria 10k
Shatt (Daju): Sudan 15k
Shoe: Chad 12k
Siamou (Seme): Burkina Faso 15k
South Gisiga: Cameroon 102k
South Koma: Ethiopia 11k
Suri: Ethiopia 10k
Swazi: South Africa 854k
Taturu (Tatoga, Mangati): Tanzania 200k
Temein: Sudan 10k
Tigon Mbembe, Tikun,: Cameroon 36k
Tira (Thiro): Sudan 40k
Tofin-Gbe: Benin 62k
Tornasi: Sudan 50k
Turkana: Ethiopia 21k
Vai (Vey, Vy): Sierra Leone 16k
Vai (Vy): Liberia 90k
Waci-Gbe: Togo 366k
Western Krahn: Cote d'Ivoire 12k
Yaka: Angola 150k
Yeye (Koba): Botswana 20k
Yoruba (Anago, Nago): Benin 393k

Pygmy
Aka Pygmy: Congo 30k
Baka Pygmy, Eastern Pygmy: Cameroon 30k
Bayaka Pygmy (Binga): Zaire 26k
Efe: Zaire 20k

Sahel-Cha
Abu Sharib: Chad 39k
Bagirmi (Lisi): Nigeria 30k
Barma (Bagirmi, Lisi): Chad 45k
Bilala: Chad 137k
Burun (Barun, Borun): Sudan 18k
Daju of Dar Dadju: Chad 23k
Daju of Dar Sila: Chad 33k
Dar Fur Daju: Sudan 70k
Dar Sila Daju: Sudan 33k
Fur (Furawi): Sudan 500k
Gule (Fung, Hameg): Sudan 17k
Gumuz (Debatsa): Sudan 40k
Ingessana (Tabi): Sudan 30k
Kenga (Kenge, Cenge): Chad 45k
Kibet, Dagel, Mourro: Chad 19k
Kimr (Gimr): Sudan 60k
Kuka: Chad 77k
Maba (Borgu, Mabang): Sudan 47k
Maba (Mabangi): Chad 150k
Mararit (Abiyi, Ebiri): Sudan 20k
Mararit, Abu Sharib: Chad 42k
Masalit: Sudan 145k, Chad 51k
Medogo (Medoga): Chad 19k
Mesakin (Masakin): Sudan 38k
Mima: Sudan 74k
Mimi (Amdang, Mututu): Chad 19k
Runga: Chad 22k, Central African Republic 15k
Sinyar (Shamya): Chad 10k
Sungor (Assagori): Sudan 15k

Sungor (Asungor): Chad 24k
Tagale (Taqalawin): Sudan 36k
Tagoi (Moreb): Sudan 13k
Tama (Gimr): Chad 63k
Tama (Tamongobo): Sudan 60k

Songhai
Dendi (Dandawa): Benin 28k
Songhai (Sonrhai): Mali 600k, Niger 390k, Nigeria 255k, Burkina Faso 123k

Soninke
Soninke (Sarakole): Mali 700k, Cote d'Ivoire 100k, Gambia 80k, Mauritania 30k
Soninke (Serahuli): Senegal 150k, Burkina Faso 90k

Susa
Susu (Soso): Guinea 722k, Sierra Leone 120k, Senegal 25k

Swahili
Bajun (Shirazi): Kenya 41k
Black African (Bantu): Saudi Arabia 205k
Comorian (Mauri,Mahor): France 90k
Comorian (Ngazija): Comoros 70k, Madagascar 69k
Segeju (Dhaiso): Kenya 58k, Tanzania 29k
Swahili: Somalia 40k, Zambia 19k, Sudan 15k, Rwanda 12k
Swahili (Coastal): Kenya 94k
Swahili (Shamba): Kenya 97k

Wolof
Wolof: Senegal 2,990k, Mali 43k, France 35k, Cote d'Ivoire 10k
Wolof (Gambian Wolof): Gambia 131k

Zerma
Zerma (Dyerma): Niger 1,495k, Nigeria 50k

Turkic Peoples

Azerbaijani
Afshari (Afsar): Iran 13,000k
Azerbaijani: Turkey 530k, Turkmenistan 386k, Kyrgyzstan 110k, Uzbekistan 38k, Ukraine 34k, Russia 16k
Azerbaijani (Azeri Turk): Azerbaijan 6,069k, Georgia 630k, Iraq 300k, Armenia 89k

Bashkir
Bashkir: Russia 1,406k, Kazakhstan 21k, Uzbekistan 21k

Kazakh
Kazakh: Kazakhstan 5,293k, China 1,112k, Uzbekistan 845k, Russia 600k, Turkmenistan 92k, Kyrgyzstan 39k, Tajikistan 12k, Ukraine 11k
Kazakh (Qazaq): Mongolia 100k

Kirghiz
Kirghiz: Kyrgyzstan 2,448k, Uzbekistan 183k, China 142k, Tajikis-

tan 67k, Russia 43k, Kazakhstan 15k

Manchu
Evenk (Tungus): Russia 12k
Evenki (Owenke, Tungus): China 10k
Manchu (Man): China 10,000k
Western Manchu (Sibo): China 27k

Mongolian
Buryat: China 65k
Buryat (Northern Mongolian): China 40k
Chinese Mongolian: China 2,713k
Dariganga: Mongolia 32k
Daur (Daguor): China 85k
Durbet (Dorwot): Mongolia 206k
Kalmyk: Russia 149k
Kalmyk-Oirat: China 139k
Khalka Mongol: China 49k
Khalkha Mongol: Mongolia 1,700k
Northern Mongolian: Mongolia 62k
Tuvinian (Tannu-Tuva): Mongolia 25k
Tuvinian (Uriankhai): Russia 166k

Other
Balkan Gagauzi Turk: Turkey 14k
Balkar: Russia 235k
Chulym (Melets Tatar): Russia 12k
Khalaj: Iran 17k
Kumyk (Kumuk, Khasav): Russia 282k
Nogay Tatar (Nogai): Russia 68k
Paongan (Pao-an, Bonan): China 12k
Salar: China 55k
Tu (Monguor, Tu-jen): China 192k
Tunghsiang: China 374k

Qashqai
Qashqai (Kashkai): Iran 850k

Tatar
Crimean Tatar: Uzbekistan 269k, Russia 26k, Romania 25k, Turkey 22k
Khakass, Sagai: Russia 57k
Nogay Tatar (Nogai): Romania 11k
Tatar: Uzbekistan 489k, Kazakhstan 343k, Ukraine 250k, Tajikistan 75k, Kyrgyzstan 73k, Turkmenistan 41k, Azerbaijan 29k, Belarus 13k
Tatar (Kazan Tatar): Russia 5,715k
Tatar (Tartar): Turkey 21k

Turkish
Anatolian Turk: Iraq 22k
Khorasani Turk: Iran 400k
Meskhetian Turk: Uzbekistan 37k
Rumelian Turk: Bulgaria 789k, Yugoslavia 250k, Bosnia-Hercegovina 50k, Romania 14k
Turk: Turkey 46,278k, Germany 1,523k, Macedonia 250k, France 214k, Netherlands 160k, Belgium 51k, Syria 45k, Australia 36k, Egypt 29k, Aus-

tria 23k, Saudi Arabia 17k, Switzerland 13k

Turkish: Kazakhstan 52k, Kyrgyzstan 22k, Azerbaijan 19k, Russia 10k

Turkish Cypriot: Cyprus 120k, United Kingdom 30k

Turkish Gypsy: Turkey 25k

Turkmen

Turkmen: Uzbekistan 131k, Syria 98k, Russia 41k, Tajikistan 14k

Turkmen (Trukhmeny): Turkmenistan 2,918k

Turkmen (Turkoman): Afghanistan 380k

Turkmen (Turkomani): Iran 722k

Uyghur

Uighur: Taiwan 26k

Uighur (Kashgar Turki): Kazakhstan 221k, Kyrgyzstan 38k, Uzbekistan 37k

Uighur (Kashgar): China 7,214k

Uzbek

Kara-Kalpak: Turkey 62k

Karachay (Alan): Russia 235k

Karakalpak: Uzbekistan 409k, Iran 36k

Northern Uzbek: Uzbekistan 15,003k

Southern Uzbek: Afghanistan 1,403k

Uzbek: Kyrgyzstan 575k, Kazakhstan 346k, Turkmenistan 331k, Russia 133k, Ukraine 21k, United States 21k, Mongolia 20k

Uzbek (Northern): Tajikistan 1,252k

Indo-Iranians of S.W. Asia

Aimaq

Aimaq-Hazara: Afghanistan 162k

Firozkohi (Char Aimaq): Afghanistan 208k

Jamshidi (Char Aimaq): Afghanistan 92k, Iran 30k

Taimani (Char Aimaq): Afghanistan 416k

Teymur (Aimaq): Iran 181k

Teymur (Timuri): Afghanistan 104k

Baluch

Eastern Baluch: Pakistan 1,735k

Southern Baluch: Pakistan 1,350k, Iran 405k, Oman 250k, United Arab Emirates 100k

Western Baluch: Turkmenistan 550k, Afghanistan 290k, Pakistan 289k, Iran 29k

Brahui

Brahui (Kur Galli): Pakistan 1,710k, Afghanistan 200k, Iran 10k

Gilaki

Gilaki: Iran 2,400k

Hazara

Hazara (Afghan Persian): Pakistan 17k

Hazara (Berberi): Afghanistan 1,403k

Hazara-Berberi (Teymur): Iran 604k

Kurd

Alevica Kurdish: Turkey 3,700k

Bajelan (Shabak, Gurani): Iraq 20k

Dimili Kurdish: Turkey 1,000k

Hawrami (Gurani): Iraq 22k

Herki: Iraq 22k, Iran 18k

Herki Kurd: Turkey 31k

Kurd: Kuwait 244k, Belgium 13k

Kurd (Kermanji): Germany 296k

Kurdish: Kazakhstan 27k, Afghanistan 23k, Kyrgyzstan 15k

Kurdish, Northern: Azerbaijan 100k

Northern Kurd: Iran 200k, France 74k, Georgia 74k

Northern Kurd (Kermanji): Turkey 3,950k, Iraq 1,457k, Lebanon 70k, Armenia 30k

Shikaki: Iran 24k, Iraq 22k

Shikaki Kurdish: Turkey 18k

Southern Kurd: Iraq 2,786k

Southern Kurd (Sorani): Iran 605k

Surchi: Iraq 11k

Western Kurd (Kermanji): Syria 668k

Luri

Luri (Lori, Feyli): Iran 4,344k

Luri (Lur): Iraq 67k

Mazanderani

Mazanderani (Tabri): Iran 2,500k

Other

Astiani: Iran 18k

Badeshi: Pakistan 14k

Bashgari (Kafar): Afghanistan 14k

Darwazi (Badakhshani): Afghanistan 10k

Deghwari: Pakistan 10k

Gurani (Bajalani): Iran 38k

Harzani: Iran 24k

Karingani: Iran 15k

Khunsari: Iran 18k

Kumzari: Oman 14k

Larestani (Lari): Iran 30k

Nangalami (Nigalami): Afghanistan 24k

Ossetian (Western Ossetian): Turkey 31k

Pashayi (Pashai): Afghanistan 162k

Pashayi, Southwestern: Afghanistan 108k

Rajkoti: Pakistan 40k

Semnani: Iran 18k

Shughni (Shugnan-Rush): Tajikistan 35k

Takistani: Iran 220k

Talysh: Iran 35k

Talysh (Lenkoran): Azerbaijan 30k

Vafsi: Iran 18k

Pathan

Eastern Pathan: United Arab Emirates 100k

Eastern Pathan (Afghan): Pakistan 11,309k

Pathan: United Kingdom 87k

Pathan (Pushtun, Afghan): Afghanistan 8,000k

Southern Pathan: Pakistan 1,000k

Western Pathan (Afghan): United Arab Emirates 102k, Iran 50k

Persian

Afghan Persian: Iran 1,691k

Iranian (Persian): United Kingdom 29k

Mussulman Tat: Iran 31k, Azerbaijan 22k

Persian: Iraq 186k, Saudi Arabia 120k, Kuwait 99k, United Arab Emirates 80k, Bahrain 65k, Oman 38k, Uzbekistan 26k, Syria 15k, Yemen 14k

Persian (Irani): Iran 22,640k, Qatar 91k, Germany 23k

Persian Bantu: Iran 3,623k

Persian, Dari: Pakistan 142k

Tajik

Afghani Tajik: Pakistan 1,000k

Afghani Tajik, Qizilb: Afghanistan 5,600k

Chinese Tajik (Tadzhiki): China 36k

Tadzhik (Persian Tajiki): Iran 60k, Kyrgyzstan 35k

Tajik: Russia 39k, Kazakhstan 27k

Tajik (Tadzhik): Tajikistan 3,345k, Uzbekistan 1,000k, China 21k

Indo-Iranians or Indo-Aryans of South Asia

Assamese

Assamese: India 13,705k, Bhutan 170k, Bangladesh 11k

Bengali

Bengali: Bangladesh 110,000k, India 68,000k, Myanmar (Burma) 236k, Pakistan 226k, United Arab Emirates 89k, Nepal 65k, Thailand 60k, Malaysia 20k, Sri Lanka 18k, Saudi Arabia 17k

Bengali (Bangla-Bhasa): United Kingdom 289k

Bengali (Hindu): Bangladesh 15,500k

Hajong (East Bengali): Bangladesh 32k, India 24k

Kayort: Nepal 22k

Kishanganjia: India 57k

Rajbansi (Tajpuri): Nepal 55k

Sylhetti Bengali: Bangladesh 6,196k, United Kingdom 104k

Tajpuri (Rajbansi): Bangladesh 13k

Bhil

Adiwasi Girasia: India 100k

Barel (Bareli): India 274k

Bauria (Babri, Bawari): India 10k

Bhilala: India 551k

Central Bhil: India 4,374k
Chodhari Bhil: India 150k
Dangs Bhil (Dangi): India 120k
Dhatki Bhil (Thar): India 15k
Dhodia (Dhobi, Doria): India 76k
Dubla: India 202k
Eastern Bhil Bhilbari: India 1,600k
Gamti (Gamit): India 136k
Mavchi (Mawachi): India 68k
Meghwar Bhil (Chamar): Pakistan
 198k
Pardhi Bhil (Paria): India 11k
Pawari Bhil: India 61k
Rajput Garasia (Dungri): India 60k
Sansi Bhil: Pakistan 14k
Tadvi Bhil (Dhanka): India 10k
Vasava: India 300k
Wagdi (Wagheri): India 1,196k

Bihari
Anga (Angika): India 424k
Bhojpuri Bihari: India 31,000k, Ne-
 pal 1,328k
Bihari: Bangladesh 1,983k, Fiji 30k
Magadhi Bihari: India 10,000k
Nagpuri Bihari: India 807k

Deccani
Deccani (Dakhini Hindi): India
 10,710k

Gond
Dhurwa (Parji, Thakar): India 90k
Dorli: India 41k
Hill Maria: India 16k
Khirwar: India 34k
Maria (Muria): India 102k
Muria (Jhoria): India 13k
SE. Gond (Koi), Gondi: India 736k
South Central Gond: India 158k

Gujarati
Gujarati: India 41,000k, Tanzania
 241k, Uganda 147k, Bangladesh 66k, Kenya 48k, Madagascar 45k, Myanmar (Burma)
 32k, Malawi 31k, Iran 24k, Malaysia 20k, Mozambique 18k,
 Zambia 12k
Gujarati (Bajania): Pakistan 849k
Patelia: India 23k

Gypsy
Arhagar Gypsy: Pakistan 14k
Baiga (Baigani, Bega): India 11k
Balkan Gypsy: Ukraine 732k,
 Moldavia 105k
Balkan Rom Gypsy: Turkey 55k,
 Iran 24k
Ghagar Rom Gypsy: Egypt 234k
Ghorbati Gypsy: Iran 80k, Iraq 50k
Gormati (Banjara, Labhan): India
 1,500k
Gypsy (Balkan): Yugoslavia 120k
Gypsy (Romani, Sinte): Yugoslavia
 31k
Halebi Gypsy (Nawari): Egypt 934k,
 Libya 33k
Indian Gypsy: India 23,668k
Kanjari (Kagari, Kangari): India 55k

Middle East Gypsy: Turkey 20k
Wogri Boli: India 19k

Hindi family
Awadhi Abadhi: Nepal 317k
Awadhi Baiswari: India 20,000k
Bangri (Deswali): India 5,000k
Binjhwari: India 49k
Bundelkhandi (Bondili): India
 8,000k
Chhattisgarhi: India 8,232k
East Indian (Hindi): Netherlands
 108k
Eastern Hindi: India 385k
Hindi: Bangladesh 400k, Pakistan
 283k, Myanmar (Burma) 115k,
 Malaysia 40k, Sri Lanka 36k,
 Tanzania 32k, Bhutan 25k, Can-
 ada 19k, Mozambique 17k
Hindi (Bazaar, Popular): India
 180,000k
Hindi, Fijian: Fiji 250k
Hindustani: India 947k
Indo-Pakistani: Zaire 125k, Saudi
 Arabia 85k, Yemen 70k, Cote
 d'Ivoire 10k
Kanauji (Western Hindi): India
 6,000k

Hindko
Kaghani: Pakistan 1,875k
Multani (Siraiki Hindi): India 20k
Northern Hindko: Pakistan 5,284k

Jat
Jat (Awan): Pakistan 14k

Kashmiri
Kashmiri: United Kingdom 116k,
 Pakistan 43k
Kashmiri (Keshur): India 3,905k

Kond
Kui (Khondi, Kond): India 1,500k
Kuvi (Khondi, Kond): India 300k

Konkani
Kanara Konkani: India 168k
Konkanese: India 4,000k

Maharathi
Berar Marathi: India 7,053k
Danuwar Rai: Nepal 10k
Dhanwar (Dhanvar): India 21k
Halbi (Bastari, Halba): India 646k
Maratha (Maharathi): India 65,000k
Thakur: India 99k

Maithili
Maitili (Maithili): India 22,000k
Maitili (Tirahutia): Nepal 1,826k

Maldivian
Maldivian (Malki): Maldives 220k

Munda-Santal
Agariya (Agria): India 12k
Bhumij (Kisan-Bhumij): India 474k
Gadaba: India 33k
Ho: India 1,250k
Juango (Puttooas): India 13k
Karmali: India 144k
Korwa (Ernga, Singli): India 14k
Mahili: India 66k
Santal (Hor, Har): Nepal 40k

Santal (Sandal, Hor): India 5,180k

Nepali-Pahari
Chameali Pahari: India 53k
Churahi Pahari: India 35k
Garhwali (Central Pahari): India
 1,277k
Jaunsari (Pahari): India 57k
Kulu Pahari (Kauli): India 172k
Kumaoni: India 2,058k
Kumaoni (Kumauni): Nepal 86k
Nepalese: Myanmar (Burma) 65k,
 Bangladesh 17k
Nepalese (Gurkhali): India 6,000k
Nepalese (Paharia): Bhutan 300k
Nepalese, Eastern: Nepal 14,900k

Newar
Newar: Nepal 500k

Oriya
Orisi (Oriya): Myanmar (Burma)
 106k
Orisi (Utkali, Vadiya): India
 33,090k, Bangladesh 13k

Other
Andh (Andha, Andhni): India 80k
Badaga: India 134k
Bagata (Bhakta): India 86k
Bateri: Pakistan 20k
Bathudi: India 105k
Bedia: India 32k
Bhadrawahi (Bhadri): India 53k
Bhattri (Bhatra): India 134k
Bhim: India 20k
Bhottara (Dhotada): India 342k
Burushas (Burusho): Pakistan 86k
Chenchu (Chenswar): India 18k
Chero: India 28k
Chik-Barik: India 30k
Dehati (Deshiya): India 38k
Gaddi (Pahari Bharmau): India 88k
Galo (Maiyon): Pakistan 200k
Gawari: India 21k
Gowlan: India 19k
Irula (Eravallon): India 50k
Jatapu: India 37k
Kamar: India 10k
Kanarese (Canarese): India 29,506k
Kanikkaran (Kani): India 10k
Kashtwari (Kistwali): India 12k
Kawar (Kamari): India 34k
Khetrani: Pakistan 14k
Kho (Chitrali, Khowar): Pakistan
 188k
Khowar (Chitrali): India 18k
Koda (Korali, Mudikor): India 175k
Kodagu (Coorg, Khurgi): India 114k
Kohistani (Garwi): Pakistan 40k
Kolai (Kohistani-Shina): Pakistan
 200k
Kolam (Kulme): India 50k
Kotia (Tribal Oriya): India 200k
Koya (Koi, Kavor): India 299k
Kurichiya: India 12k
Kuruba (Urali): India 700k
Kurumba (Southern Kannada): India
 10k

Laccadive Mappilla: India 50k
Limbu (Monpa): Bhutan 25k
Lodhi (Lodha): India 44k
Majhwar: India 28k
Malvi (Ujjaini, Malavi): India 1,806k
Manjhi: India 19k
Mukha-Dora (Reddi): India 10k
Nahari: India 19k
Od (Oad): Pakistan 30k
Pahari: India 28k
Pahari Mandeali: India 358k
Panika: India 31k
Porja (Konda-Dora): India 16k
Punjabi Pahari: Pakistan 14k
Sadri: Bangladesh 39k
Saharia (Sor): India 174k
Shin (Sina, Dardi): India 20k
Shina (Dras, Shin): Pakistan 300k
Shumashti: Pakistan 14k
Sinhalese (Singhalese): Sri Lanka 13,215k
Sonha: Nepal 10k
Tangchangya: Bangladesh 18k
Tipera (Tripuri): Bangladesh 54k
Turvali: Pakistan 60k
Western Punjabi: Afghanistan 23k
Yanadi (Yadi): India 205k
Yerukala (Erukala): India 113k

Panjabi
Dogri (Hindi Dogri): India 2,165k
Eastern Punjabi: India 20,000k
Kahluri Pahari: India 66k
Mirpur Punjabi: India 947k
Punjabi: Sri Lanka 92k, Malaysia 80k, Myanmar (Burma) 54k, Tanzania 33k, Iran 24k, Oman 22k, Thailand 20k, Kenya 10k, Bangladesh 10k
Southern Punjabi: Pakistan 20,000k
Western Punjabi: Pakistan 65,000k

Rajasthan
Bagri: India 1,759k, Pakistan 100k
Bhattiana (Bhatneri): Pakistan 14k
Dhatki Marwari (Bhil): Pakistan 200k
Gujar (Gujuri, Kashmiri): India 1,600k
Gujur Rajasthani: Afghanistan 17k
Gujuri Rajasthani: Pakistan 300k
Harauti (Hadauti): India 886k
Khandeshi: India 207k
Marwari: Pakistan 85k
Mina: India 900k
Nimadi (Nimari): India 834k
Parkari Kachchhi: Pakistan 150k
Rajasthani (Marwari): India 9,452k
Sondwari: India 32k
Southern Marwari: Pakistan 50k

Sindhi
Balmiki: Pakistan 25k
Cutch (Kachchi, Cutch): India 619k
Cutchi Indian: Kenya 10k
Cutchi Indian (Kohli): Tanzania 652k
Kutchi Kohli (Lohar): Pakistan 50k

Sindhi: Pakistan 14,000k, Malaysia 20k, Afghanistan 12k
Sindhi (Kachchi): India 2,400k
Tharadari Koli: Pakistan 30k
Wadiyara Koli: Pakistan 75k

Tamil Moor
Ceylon Moor: Sri Lanka 1,200k

Tharu
Chitwan Tharu: Nepal 30k
Dang Tharu (Dangha): Nepal 259k
Deokri Tharu: Nepal 80k
Mahotari Tharu: Nepal 32k
Saptari Tharu: Nepal 60k

Tulu
Tulu (Tullu, Thulu): India 2,000k

Urdu
Indo-Mauritian (Urdu): Mauritius 26k
Southern Uzbek: Pakistan 566k
Urdu: Pakistan 8,000k, South Africa 170k, United States 129k, Oman 41k, Saudi Arabia 34k, Qatar 28k, Bahrain 27k, Turkey 18k, Germany 16k, Canada 14k, Malaysia 10k
Urdu (Hindi): Afghanistan 12k
Urdu (Islami, Undri): India 43,000k
Urdu (Islami, Undri, Urudu): Iran 60k

Thai & Dai Peoples
Khmer
Cambodian (Central Khmer): Laos 10k
Center Khmer: Vietnam 895k
Central Khmer: Cambodia (Kampuchea) 7,500k, Thailand 320k
Khmer (Cambodian): France 53k
Northern Khmer: Thailand 1,000k

Lao
Lao (Laotian Tai): Laos 2,815k, Cambodia (Kampuchea) 55k, Vietnam 10k

Li
Li (Paoting): China 747k

Lu
Lu (Pai-I): China 250k
Lu (Tai Lu, Lue): Myanmar (Burma) 200k

Other
Brao (Proue, Love): Laos 18k
Bru: Laos 50k
Bulang (Pula, Samtao): China 24k
Flowery Meo: China 1,000k
Flowery Meo (Miao Hwa): Vietnam 160k
Golden Palaung: China 24k
Golden Palaung (Shwe): Myanmar (Burma) 150k
Hkun (Khun Shan): Myanmar (Burma) 14k
Hkun (Khun): Thailand 100k
Ir: Laos 10k
Kang: China 37k
Kantu (High Katu): Laos 19k

Katang (Kataang): Laos 10k
Khao: Vietnam 10k
Khmu: Thailand 29k, Vietnam 16k
Kui (Suei): Thailand 650k
Kui (Sui, Old Khmer): Laos 57k
Lamet (Lemet): Laos 10k
Lao Phuan: Laos 109k, Thailand 75k
Lao Song (Song): Thailand 20k
Lor: Laos 10k
Lu: Thailand 50k, Laos 16k
Man Cao Lan: Vietnam 114k, China 72k
Mnong, Central: Vietnam 67k
Mnong, Eastern: Vietnam 48k
Mon (Talaing, Mun): Myanmar (Burma) 1,053k
Muong (Thang, Wang): Vietnam 914k
Nhang (Giang, Dioi): Vietnam 38k
Nhang (Nyang, Dioi): China 258k
Nyaw (Yo): Thailand 50k
Nyong: Thailand 12k
Ongbe (Be): China 520k
Oy (Riyao): Laos 11k
Pacoh: Vietnam 15k
Pacoh (Bo): Laos 21k
Palaung (Bonglong): China 17k
Phu Thai (Phuthai): Laos 100k
Phuthai (Puthai): Thailand 50k
Red Tai (Thai Deng): Vietnam 100k
Red Tai (Tribal Tai): Laos 25k
Riang-Lang (Black Yang): Myanmar (Burma) 20k
Rumai: Myanmar (Burma) 139k
Saek (Sek): Thailand 25k
Saek (Tai Sek): Laos 28k
Shui (Sui): China 346k
Silver Palaung: Myanmar (Burma) 71k
So: Thailand 50k
So (Kah So, So Makon): Laos 80k
Stieng (Budip): Cambodia (Kampuchea) 28k
Talaing (Mon, Peguan): Thailand 70k
Thai Nung: Laos 47k
Tho (Tai Tho): China 122k
Tho (Tai Tho, Tay): Vietnam 1,191k
Tung (Dong, Kam): China 2,388k
Upper Ta-Oy (Kantua): Vietnam 26k
Upper Taoih (Taoy): Laos 37k
Western Bru (Baru): Thailand 20k
Western Bru (Vankieu): Laos 20k
Western Lawa: China 75k
White Tai (Thai Trang): Vietnam 400k, Laos 38k, United States 10k

Puyi
Chienchiang: China 122k
Puyi (Bouyei, Pu-I): China 2,696k

Shan
Burmese Shan: Myanmar (Burma) 2,500k
Chinese Shan: Laos 20k
Chinese Shan (Dai Nue): China 250k
Chinese Shan (Tai Neu): Myanmar (Burma) 72k

Khamti Shan (Khampti): Myanmar (Burma) 70k
Shan (Great Thai): Thailand 30k
Shan (Tai Yay, Sha): China 237k
Yunnanese Shan (Dai): China 1,025k

Shuang
Yung-Chuun: China 12k
Zhuang (Chuang, Chwan): China 10,000k

Tai Dan
Black Tai (Tai Dam): Thailand 20k
Black Tai (Thai Den): Vietnam 550k, China 20k
Black Tai (Tribal Tai): Laos 100k

Tai-Nung
Highland Nung Tai Nun: Vietnam 705k
Thai Nung (Nong): China 100k

Thai
Central Thai: Thailand 18,300k
Han Chinese: Thailand 477k
Khon-Thai: Myanmar (Burma) 14k
Northern Tai (Yuan, Phyap): Thailand 6,005k
Southern Tai: Thailand 5,000k
Thai: Malaysia 20k
Thai (Central Tai): Laos 144k, Cambodia (Kampuchea) 26k
Tsun-Lao: Vietnam 37k

Sino-Tibetan Peoples of E. Asia & Himalayas

Bhutanese
Bhutanese (Bhotia): Bhutan 200k
Central Bhotia: Bhutan 353k
Dakpa (Sagtengpa): Bhutan 68k
Eastern Bhotia: Bhutan 300k
Sangla: Bhutan 80k
Sikkimese Bhotia: India 35k

Burmese
Arakanese (Maghi): India 12k
Burmese: Bangladesh 100k, Thailand 60k, United Kingdom 12k
Burmese (Myen, Bhama): Myanmar (Burma) 27,176k, India 47k, Malaysia 20k
Chaungtha: Myanmar (Burma) 122k
Intha: Myanmar (Burma) 141k
Maghi (Arakanese, Mogh): Myanmar (Burma) 517k
Taungyo (Dawe): Myanmar (Burma) 443k
Yangbye (Yangye): Myanmar (Burma) 1,022k

Chinese
Han Chinese: Nepal 47k, Tanzania 15k
Han Chinese (Cantonese): Laos 48k
Han Chinese (Hainanese): China 5,501k
Han Chinese (Hakka): China 25,725k
Han Chinese (Hunanese): China 42,751k

Han Chinese (Mandarin): North Korea 168k, Laos 25k
Han Chinese, Ch. Nung: China 54,965k

Chinese-Hui
Dungan (Hui, Huizui): Kyrgyzstan 39k, Kazakhstan 31k
Hui (Chinese Muslim): China 7,203k

Gurung
Eastern Gurung: Nepal 60k
Galle Gurung (Ghale): Nepal 12k
Western Gurung (Manang): Nepal 90k

Hmong
Red Meo (Meo Do): Vietnam 149k

Japanese
Japanese: Japan 121,050k, Thailand 10k
Japanese (Nihongo): China 12k
Kunigami: Japan 123k
Northern Amami-Oshima: Japan 75k
Oki-no-erabu: Japan 18k
Southern Amami-Oshima: Japan 16k
Southern Ryukyuan: Japan 67k
Toku-no-shima: Japan 38k
Yayeyama: Japan 47k

Korean
Korean: North Korea 23,800k, Russia 112k

Magar
Eastern Magar (Gurkha): Nepal 290k
Kham-Magar (Kham): Nepal 15k
Magar (Eastern Magar): Bhutan 17k
Western Magar: Nepal 210k

Manipuri
Manipuri (Meithei): India 1,171k, Bangladesh 131k
Manipuri (Ponna): Myanmar (Burma) 23k

Other
Adi (Miri): China 61k
Adi (Miri, Mishing): India 470k
Adi-Galo (Galong): India 37k
Apatani: India 13k
Athpare Rai: Nepal 230k
Atsi (Szi, Atsi-Maru): Myanmar (Burma) 13k
Bai (Pai, Minchia): China 900k
Bangni, Nissi, Dafla: India 174k
Bantawa Rai: Nepal 35k
Biyo: China 100k
Cambodian Cham (Western Cham): Laos 14k
Cham, Eastern: Vietnam 80k
Chamlinge Rai: Nepal 30k
Chinese (Fuchow): Thailand 10,537k
Chinese (Hokkien): Thailand 1,082k
Deori (Deuri): India 15k
Dimasa (Kachari): India 70k
Gamale Kham: Nepal 10k
Hallam: Myanmar (Burma) 100k
Han Chinese, Hokkien: Taiwan 14,178k
Hani: Vietnam 20k
Hani, Ho-Nhi: China 500k

Iu Mein: China 200k
Jinuo (Youle): China 18k
Jyarung (Rgyarong): China 100k
Kabui: India 50k
Kado (Asak, Thet): Myanmar (Burma) 129k
Kado (Sak, Thet): China 100k
Kalinge Rai: Nepal 10k
Kiutze (Chopa): India 57k
Koch: India 35k
Koch (Banai, Konch): Bangladesh 53k
Kulunge Rai (Pelmung): Nepal 15k
Lalung: India 11k
Lashi (Letsi, Acye): Myanmar (Burma) 56k
Lasi (Chashan): China 37k
Lepcha (Rong): India 24k
Lhoba: India 202k
Limbu: Nepal 254k
Limbu (Monpa): India 24k
Loba (Mustang): Nepal 20k
Mahei (Mahe, Mabe): China 12k
Malu (Lansu, Diso): China 13k
Maring: India 11k
Mech, Boro, Bodo, Bod: India 600k
Mru (Mro): Myanmar (Burma) 34k, Bangladesh 18k
Mru (Niopreng, Mrung): India 15k
Muei Tai: Laos 24k
Nakhi (Na-Hsi, Moso): China 278k
Nocte: India 40k
Norra (Nora, Noza): Myanmar (Burma) 10k
Northeastern Tai (Isan): Thailand 13,300k
Nung (Anoong, Nu, Lu): Myanmar (Burma) 19k
Pao: India 24k
Phunoi: Thailand 32k
Pumi: China 30k
Punoi: Laos 19k
Riang: India 126k
Saam Rai: Nepal 43k
Sherpa (Sharpa Bhotia): Nepal 14k, India 10k
Sila: Laos 22k
Sunwar (Sunbar): Nepal 20k
Tamachhange Rai: Nepal 43k
Taman: Myanmar (Burma) 10k
Thulunge Rai: Nepal 25k
Tipera (Tripuri): India 502k
Tripuri: Bangladesh 50k
Western (Cambodian) Cham: Cambodia (Kampuchea) 195k
Yakha: Nepal 20k
Yi, Central: China 200k

Tibetan
Amdo: China 810k
Atuentse: China 590k
Balti (Baltistani Bhotia): India 40k
Baltistani Bhotia: Pakistan 270k
Burig (Bhotia): India 132k
Burig (Purig Bhotia): China 185k
Burig (Purig-pa): Pakistan 368k
Chepang (Tsepang): Nepal 18k

Chiang (Qiang): China 130k
Choni (Northern Tibetan): China
24k
Groma: India 14k, China 12k
Helambu Sherpa: Nepal 10k
Kanauri (Kanawari): India 60k
Kham (Khams Bhotia): China 1,446k
Ladakhi: China 12k
Ladakhi (Ladaphi): India 95k
Lahuli (Tinan): India 11k
Men-pa: China 30k
Mugali: Nepal 35k
Ngolok (Golog): China 80k
Panang: China 12k
Rabha (Maitaria): India 200k
Sulung: China 49k
Thami: Nepal 20k
Tibetan (Bhotia): Nepal 60k
Tibetan (Lhasa): India 100k
Tseku: China 12k

Yao
Highland Yao (Myen): Vietnam
474k, Laos 50k
Punu (Bunu, Yuno): China 339k
Yao (Highland Yao): Thailand 34k

Malay Peoples

Acehnese
Aceh: Indonesia 3,100k
Simeulue: Indonesia 130k

Bali-Sasak
Bali: Indonesia 350k
Sasak (Lombok): Indonesia 2,000k
Sumbawa: Indonesia 300k

Batak
Alas-Kluet: Indonesia 80k
Batak Mandailing: Indonesia 400k
Gayo (Gajo): Indonesia 200k

Borneo-Kalimantan
Bakumpai: Indonesia 40k
Bisayan Tutong: Brunei 17k
Brunei (Kedeyan): Brunei 83k
Dohoi: Indonesia 105k
Kendayan Dayak: Indonesia 140k
Kinabatangan Sungai: Malaysia 10k
Lawangan: Indonesia 100k
Makian, Barat: Indonesia 12k
Makian, Timur: Indonesia 20k
Modang: Indonesia 15k
Selako Dayak: Indonesia 100k
Siang: Indonesia 79k
Tidung (Nonukan): Malaysia 25k

Bugi & Makassarese
Bentong: Indonesia 25k
Buginese: Malaysia 568k
Bugis: Indonesia 3,300k
Campalagian (Tasing): Indonesia
30k
Duri: Indonesia 95k
Enkerang: Indonesia 50k
Konjo, Pengunungan: Indonesia
150k
Konjo, Pesisir: Indonesia 120k
Maiwa: Indonesia 50k
Makasar: Indonesia 1.500k

Mamuju (Udai): Indonesia 60k
Mandar: Indonesia 200k
Pattae': Indonesia 15k
Salajarese: Indonesia 90k
Ulumandak (Ulunda): Indonesia 31k

Gorontalo
Bolango: Indonesia 23k
Buol (Bual): Indonesia 75k
Gorontalese (Wau): Indonesia 800k
Kaidipan: Indonesia 24k
Suwawa: Indonesia 13k

Javanese
Cirebon: Indonesia 2,200k
Jawa, Banumasan: Indonesia 5,810k
Jawa, Jawara: Indonesia 6,800k
Jawa, Pasisir Kulon: Indonesia
2,850k
Jawa, Pasisir Lor: Indonesia 20,000k
Osing: Indonesia 350k
Osing Jawa: Indonesia 350k
Tenggerese: Indonesia 500k

Komering-Lampung
Abung: Indonesia 500k
Komering (Njo): Indonesia 800k
Lampungese (Lampongerese): Indo-
nesia 2,000k
Pubian: Indonesia 410k

Madurese
Madura: Indonesia 12,500k

Malay
Aji: Indonesia 40k
Baba Chinese Creole: Malaysia
381k, Singapore 15k
Banjar Melau: Indonesia 2.567k
Banjarese (Banjar Melau): Malaysia
3,000k
Batin: Indonesia 70k
Bazaar Low Malay Creole: Malaysia
40k, Singapore 28k
Indonesian: Malaysia 200k, Philip-
pines 35k, Singapore 29k,
Saudi Arabia 17k
Malay: Yemen 28k, Myanmar
(Burma) 23k, Madagascar 16k,
Taiwan 11k
Malay (Javar): Sri Lanka 50k
Malay (Melaja): Brunei 22k
Malay (Melaju): Thailand 477k, Phil-
ippines 140k
Malay (Melaju, Melayu): Malaysia
7,181k
Malay, Negeri Sembili: Malaysia
300k
Malaysian Malay: United Kingdom
47k
Melayu, Belide: Indonesia 20k
Melayu, Berau: Indonesia 20k
Melayu, Daya: Indonesia 50k
Melayu, Dayak: Indonesia 520k
Melayu, Deli: Indonesia 4.000k
Melayu, Sambas: Indonesia 280k
Pattani Malay: Thailand 1,000k
Tenggarang Kutai: Indonesia 270k

Malay-Sumatra
Bengkulu: Indonesia 55k

Enim: Indonesia 70k
Kaur: Indonesia 50k
Kayu Agung: Indonesia 45k
Kelingi: Indonesia 50k
Kerinchi (Mokomoko): Indonesia
280k
Kubu (Orang Darat): Indonesia 10k
Lematang: Indonesia 150k
Lembak (Oran Sindang): Indonesia
150k
Lintang: Indonesia 70k
Lubu: Indonesia 39k
Melayu, Bangka: Indonesia 200k
Melayu, Belitung: Indonesia 170k
Melayu, Riau: Indonesia 2,000k
Melayu-Jambi: Indonesia 650k
Musi: Indonesia 130k
Ogan: Indonesia 300k
Palembangese: Indonesia 620k
Pasemah: Indonesia 450k
Penesak: Indonesia 20k
Ranau: Indonesia 60k
Rawas: Indonesia 150k
Riau Malay: Malaysia 80k
Sekayu: Indonesia 250k
Semendau (Malay, Semendo): Indo-
nesia 105k

Minangkabau-Rejang
Minangkabau: Malaysia 9,818k
Minangkabau (Padang): Indonesia
8,000k
Muko-Muko: Indonesia 30k
Pekal: Indonesia 30k
Rejang: Indonesia 700k

Other
Bimanese: Indonesia 440k
Gesa (Geser-Goram): Indonesia 38k
Haruku: Indonesia 18k
Jakun (Djakun): Malaysia 10k
Kei (Tanimbarese): Indonesia 88k
Lowland Semang: Indonesia 10k
Malagasy Maore: Comoros 12k
Northern Sakai (Pie): Malaysia 12k
Northern Sinama: Malaysia 30k
Sanana (Sula, Facei): Indonesia 25k
Tamiang: Indonesia 30k
Ternate (Tematan): Indonesia 47k
Toala': Indonesia 38k
Tontemboan: Indonesia 150k
Wewewa (W. Sumbanese): Indone-
sia 100k

Philippine Tribal
Albay Bicolano (Buhi): Philippines
480k
Ayangan Ifugao (Batad): Philippines
52k
Bilaan (Blaan): Philippines 200k
Binukid: Philippines 100k
Cataelano Mandaya: Philippines 19k
Cotabato Manobo: Philippines 15k
Ifugao Amganad: Philippines 27k
Inlaod Itneg: Philippines 14k
Kalagan, Tagakaulu: Philippines 38k
Kankanaey (Northern): Philippines
70k

Lubuagan Kalinga: Philippines 40k
Manobo, Agusan: Philippines 40k
Manobo, Dibabawon: Philippines 10k
Manobo, Matig Salug: Philippines 30k
Manobo, Sarangani: Philippines 35k
Manobo, Western Bukid: Philippines 10k
Mayoyao Ifugao: Philippines 16k
Obo Manobo: Philippines 10k
Palawano, Central: Philippines 12k
Sambal Botolan: Philippines 32k
Southern Itneg: Philippines 14k
Southern Kalinga: Philippines 12k
Subanon, Lapuyan: Philippines 25k
Subanon, Sindangan: Philippines 80k
T'boli: Philippines 80k
Tagabawa Manobo, Bago: Philippines 40k
Tiruray: Philippines 40k
Tuboy Subanon: Philippines 10k
Villaviciosa Agta: Philippines 14k

S. Philippine & Borneo Muslims
Bajau (Sea Gypsy): Indonesia 50k, Philippines 40k
Bajau Kagayan: Philippines 15k
Bisaya (Sabah Bisaya): Malaysia 10k
Central Sama: Philippines 100k
Central Sama (Sinama): Malaysia 40k
Kalagan: Philippines 20k
Magindanaw (Ilanum): Philippines 1,000k
Mapun Sama (Jama Mapun): Philippines 15k
Northern Sinama: Philippines 60k
Pangutaran Sama: Philippines 20k
Southern Sama: Philippines 30k
Southern Sama (Bajau): Malaysia 20k
Tausug (Moro Joloano): Philippines 652k
Tausug (Sulu, Suluk): Malaysia 110k
West Coast Bajau: Malaysia 50k, Brunei 10k
Yakan (Yacan): Philippines 106k

Sulawesi-C
Bungku: Indonesia 22k
Butonese: Malaysia 24k
Cia-Cia: Indonesia 15k
Dampelas: Indonesia 13k
Kulisusu: Indonesia 23k
Muna (Wuna): Indonesia 230k
Pancana (Kapontori): Indonesia 15k
Toli-toli: Indonesia 28k
Tomini: Indonesia 44k
Tukangbesi Selatan: Indonesia 130k
Tukangbesi Utara: Indonesia 120k
Wawonii: Indonesia 22k
Wolio: Indonesia 30k

Sundanese
Banten: Indonesia 500k
Sunda: Indonesia 32,000k

Eurasian Peoples

Albanian
Albanian: Albania 1,652k
Albanian (Shqip): Egypt 18k
Albanian, Tosk: Albania 1,248k
Gheg: Yugoslavia 715k

Bosnian
Bosnian: Turkey 20k
Bosnian (Muslimani): Yugoslavia 8,900k, Bosnia-Hercegovina 1,300k, Croatia 143k, Serbia 93k, Macedonia 38k

N.Caucasus
Abaza: Russia 29k
Abazinian, Abaza: Turkey 15k
Agul (Aguly, Koshan): Russia 19k
Andi (Qwannab): Russia 10k
Avar: Azerbaijan 46k
Avar (Dagestani): Russia 550k
Chechen, Shishan: Kazakhstan 52k
Chechen, Shishan,: Russia 939k
Circassian: Turkey 71k, Syria 25k
Circassian (Cherkess): Jordan 44k
Darghinian (Dargwa): Russia 369k
East Circassian: Russia 46k
East Circassian (Kabardian): Turkey
Ingush: Kazakhstan 21k
Ingush (Galgai, Ingush): Russia 230k
Kabardian: Saudi Arabia 17k
Lak (Laki, Kumux): Russia 112k
Lezgian (Lezghi): Russia 189k, Azerbaijan 158k
Rutul (Rutal, Mukhad): Russia 20k
Tabasaran (Ghumghum): Russia 95k
Tsakhur (Caxur): Azerbaijan 14k
West Circassian: Russia 125k

Other
Corsican: France 200k
Gascon: France 202k
Jat (Jati, Jatu): Russia 50k, Ukraine 32k
Mingrelian (Laz, Zan): Turkey 30k
Pomak: Greece 30k

Siberian & Arctic
Chukchi (Chukot): Russia 13k
Khanti (Ostyak, Ostiak): Russia 14k
Udmurt (Votyak): Russia 534k
Yakut: Russia 400k
Yurak Samoyed (Nenets): Russia 27k

Jewish

Jews
Arabic Jewish: Israel 144k
Bombay Jew (Bney Israel): India 12k
Caucasian Mountain Jew: Russia 15k
Central Asian Jew: Uzbekistan 30k
Dutch Jewish: Netherlands 20k
Falasha (Black Jew): Israel 2,782k
French Jew: Israel 2,782k
Georgian Jew: Georgia 10k
German Jew: Canada 341k, Israel 225k, Mexico 52k
Israeli Jew: United States 3,122k
Israeli Jewish: Israel 2,782k

Jewish: Russia 1,866k, Argentina 702k, Ukraine 509k, United Kingdom 434k, Canada 340k, Brazil 330k, Latvia 258k, France 229k, Iran 120k, Belarus 117k, Romania 113k, Australia 107k, Hungary 105k, Moldavia 72k, Uzbekistan 69k, Mexico 68k, Uruguay 57k, Italy 41k, Belgium 39k, Chile 35k, Azerbaijan 26k, Kazakhstan 20k, Sweden 16k, Lithuania 13k, Turkey 12k, Zimbabwe 11k, Georgia 11k, Tajikistan 10k
Jewish (Judeo-German): United States 2,041k
Jewish Tat (Judeo-Tat): Iran 30k
Judeo-Persian: Iran 198k
Maghrebi Jewish: Israel 2,782k
Morrocan Jew: Morocco 23k
Portuguese Jewish: Netherlands 15k
Romanian Jew: Israel 2,782k
Russian Jew: Israel 2,782k
Spanish Jew: Israel 135k, Argentina 17k

Other

Mexican Indigenous
Huichol: Mexico 20k
Jacalteco, Western: Mexico 11k
Mixe, Noreste: Mexico 21k
Mixteco Atatlahuaca: Mexico 12k
Mixteco, Metlatonoc: Mexico 60k
Nahuatl Sur de Puebla: Mexico 50k
Nahuatl, Central: Mexico 63k
Nahuatl, Southeast: Mexico 130k
Tarahumara, Oeste: Mexico 15k
Tepehua, Northern: Mexico 15k
Tojolabal: Mexico 36k
Tzotzil Carranza: Mexico 10k
Zapateco Eastern Tlacolula: Mexico 11k
Zapoteco Quiatoni: Mexico 11k
Zapoteco Rincon Sur: Mexico 12k
Zoque Copainala: Mexico 10k
Zoque Francisco Leon: Mexico 20k

New Guinea
Bunak (Mare): Indonesia 71k
Imbongu (Imbon Ggo): Papua New Guinea 16k
Ternatese (Ternatan): Indonesia 47k

Other
Buin (Uitai, Uisai): Papua New Guinea 18k
Mam, Tajumulco: Guatemala 35k
Papago: United States 15k
Surinamese Aucan: Netherlands 15k

S. American Indigenous
Chiriguano: Bolivia 15k
Guajaro: Colombia 135k
Quichua, Highland, Canar: Ecuador 100k
Shuar (Jivaro): Ecuador 30k
Warrau: Venezuela 18k
Yanomamo: Venezuela 12k

Suggested Resources

Several of the following resources may be found or ordered through your local Christian bookstore or missions resource centre. Many of these books are available through William Carey Library Publishers at the U.S. Center for World Mission (1-800-MISSION, 1-800-647-7466, or 1-818-798-0819). William Carey Library Publishers also has a wide variety of other books and materials you may find helpful. Write for a free resource catalogue: PO Box 40129, Pasadena, CA 91104, USA.

Resources for Praying through the Window

10/40 Window Video for Children and *Prayerwalking for Kids*, Joey and Fawn Paris, 6673 Sora Street, Ventura, CA 93003, USA. Phone: 1-805-650-3511.

Light the Window – a video which focuses on the 100 Gateway Cities of the 10/40 Window with an emphasis on prayer and prayer journeys. Revised edition, 1996. Christian Broadcasting Network and Caleb Project. Internet: info@cproject.com, Phone: 1-303-730-4170.

Prayer Journeys, A Leader's How-To Manual. Compiled by John Hanna, 1995. Caleb Project. Internet: info@cproject.com, Phone: 1-303-730-4170.

Prayerwalking: A New Approach to Spiritual Warfare. Graham Kendrick and John Houghton, 1990. Kingsway Publications (UK).

Prayerwalking: Praying On-Site with Insight. Steve Hawthorne and Graham Kendrick, 1993. Creation House, Lake Mary, FL. Phone: 1-800-451-4598.

Praying through the 100 Gateway Cities of the 10/40 Window. C. Peter Wagner, Stephen Peters, and Mark Wilson, 1995, AD2000 and Beyond, YWAM Publishing, Seattle. Available through Caleb Project. Phone: 1-303-730-4170.

Praying through the Window I – Countries of the 10/40 Window prayer guide. Available through Caleb Project. Internet: info@cproject.com, Phone: 1-303-730-4170.

Strongholds of the 10/40 Window. Edited by George Otis, Jr., YWAM Publishing, PO Box 55787, Seattle, WA 98155, USA. Phone: 1-800-922-2143 or 1-206-771-1153.

To the Ends of the Earth – a video focusing on the unreached peoples of the 10/40 Window. 1996, Christian Broadcasting Network and Caleb Project. Internet: info@cproject.com, Phone: 1-303-730-4170.

The WindoWatchman. Michael Ebert, ed., 1994. Christian Information Network, 11025 State Highway 83, Colorado Springs, CO 80921. Phone: 1-719-522-1040.

Wisdom for the Window: Practical Training for Prayer Journeyers. Videos by Steve Hawthorne. Christian Information Network, 11025 State Highway 83, Colorado Springs, CO 80921. Phone: 1-719-522-1040.

Resources on Prayer

The Believers' Guide to Spiritual Warfare. Tom White, 1990. Servant Publications, PO Box 8617, Ann Arbor, MI 48107.

The Last of the Giants. George Otis, Jr., 1991. Chosen Books, Baker Bookhouse, Grand Rapids.

Mighty Prevailing Prayer. Wesley Duewel, 1990. Zondervan Publishing, Grand Rapids.

Prayer Warrior Series. C. Peter Wagner. Available through The Arsenal, Global Harvest Ministries. Phone: 1-800-772-7097 or 1-719-262-9929.

Power through Prayer. E. M. Bounds, 1972. Baker Books, Grand Rapids.

Touch the World through Prayer. Wesley Duewel, 1986. Zondervan, Grand Rapids.

With Concerts of Prayer: Christians Join for Spiritual Awakening and World Evangelization. David Bryant, 1984. Regal Books, Ventura, CA 93006.

Resources on Missions

Adoption: A Practical Guide to Successfully Adopting an Unreached People Group. Edited by Bruce Camp. William Carey Library Publishers, PO Box 40129, Pasadena, CA 91104, USA, Phone: 1-800-MISSION or 1-818-798-0819, Fax: 1-818-794-0477.

Catch the Vision 2000. Bill & Amy Stearns, 1991. Bethany House Publishers, Minneapolis. Phone: 1-612-829-2500.

A Clouded Future: Advancing North American World Missions. James F. Engel, 1996, Christian Stewardship Association, 3195 S. Superior, Suite 303, Milwaukee, WI 53207, USA. Phone: 1-414-483-1945.

Doing Your Bit, Video, 1991, William Carey Library Publishers, PO Box 40129, Pasadena, CA 91104, USA, Phone: 1-800-MISSION or 1-818-798-0819, Fax: 1-818-794-0477.

Destination 2000 (a video Bible study on missions). Bob Sjogren. Available through Frontier Associates, 325 North Stapley Road, Mesa, AZ 85203, USA. Phone: 1-800-GO2-THEM.

Exploring the Land: Discovering Ways for Unreached Peoples to Follow Christ. Shane Bennett & Kim Felder, with Steve Hawthorne, 1995. Caleb Project. Phone: 1-303-730-4170.

Global Countdown 2000. 4 Videos, 1995, U.S. Center for World Mission.

The Great Omission. Robertson McQuilkin, 1984. Baker Books, Grand Rapids.

Let the Nations Be Glad. John Piper, 1993. Baker Books, Grand Rapids.

Mission Frontiers: Bulletin of the U.S. Center for World Mission. Published six times a year by the U.S. Center for World Mission, Pasadena. Phone: 1-818-798-2236.

Mission Today '95: An Annual Overview of the World of Missions. 1995, Berry Publishing Services, Inc., Evanston, IL. Phone: 1-708-869-1573.

Perspectives on the World Christian Movement. A missions-survey course offered around the nation and around the world. Call 1-818-398-2125 for more information.

Spiritual Leadership. J. Oswald Sanders, 1967. Moody Bible Institute, Chicago.

START I & II – Examining the Bible to Discover God's Global Purpose. Caleb Project. Phone: 1-303-730-4170.

Unveiled At Last: Discover God's Hidden Message from Genesis to Revelation. YWAM Publishing, PO Box 55787, Seattle, WA 98155, USA. Phone: 1-800-922-2143 or 1-206-771-1153.

Vision for the Nations: Catching God's Heart for All Peoples. 1996, William Carey Library Publishers, PO Box 40129, Pasadena, CA 91104, USA, Phone: 1-800-MISSION or 1-818-798-0819, Fax: 1-818-794-0477.

What in the World is God Doing?: The Essentials of Global Missions. C. Gordon Olson, 1994. Global Gospel Publishers.

Resources on Peoples

Adopt-a-People Clearing House. 721 N. Tejon, PO Box 1795, Colorado Springs, CO 80901. Phone: 1-719-473-8800.

Bethany World Prayer Center. Attn: Unreached Peoples Project, 13855 Plank Rd, Baker, LA 70714, USA. Phone: 1-504-774-2000, Fax: 1-504-774-2001,Internet: 102132.52@Compuserve.com.

Global Prayer Digest. Published twelve times a year by Frontier Fellowship, 1605 Elizabeth Street, Pasadena, CA 91104. Phone: 1-818-398-2249.

Muslim Peoples: A World Ethnographic Survey. Richard Weekes, ed., 1984.

Operation World, 5th Edition. Patrick Johnstone, 1993. Zondervan Publishing, Grand Rapids.

Specific people-group information — sheets, videos, prayer guides, and strategy reports – more than 15 people groups that Caleb Project teams have researched since 1987, including the Azerbaijani, Turkmen, Kazaks, Malay, and Uzbeks. Caleb Project. Phone: 1-303-730-4170.

You Can Change the World. The children's version of *Operation World.* Jill Johnstone, 1993. Zondervan Publishing, Grand Rapids.

Resources for Missions Mobilisation

ACMC: Advancing Churches in Missions Commitment. PO Box ACMC, Wheaton, IL 60189-8000. 1-708-260-1660.

Adopt-a-People Campaign. U.S. Center for World Mission, 1605 Elizabeth St., Pasadena, CA 91104. 1-818-398-2200.

Brigada-orgs-missionmobilizers, an internet email conference. E-mail natewilson@xc.org for more information.

Kidscan Network Catalog. 445 Webster Drive, York, PA 17402, USA. Phone: 1-800-543-7554, Fax: 1-717-757-6103, Internet: kidscan@aol.com.

Make a Difference: How to Mobilize Your Church to New Mission Vision. A 4-Session, 4-Hour Program to Train Mission Mobilizers. Bill and Amy Stearns. 1996, ProclaMedia, 5050 Edison, Colorado Springs, CO 80915, USA.

Run With the Vision. Bill and Amy Stearns. 1995, Bethany House.

Serving as Senders: How to Care for Your Missionaries. Neal Pirolo, 1991. Emmaus Road International, San Diego.

A Sunday for the World: A Complete Missions Awareness Program. Bill Stearns, 1996, Gospel Light Publishing, 2300 Knoll Dr., Ventura, CA 93003, USA. Phone: 1-800-446-7735 or 1-805-644-9721.

World Missions Skits & Dramas. Caleb Project. Phone: 1-303-730-4170.

Internet Resources

AD2000: http://www.ad2000.org/ — Information on AD2000 initiatives and unreached people groups.

Advance: A free monthly missions newsletter with prayer requests and praises. Request a subscription from Mark Kelly, Internet: 70420.1057@Compuserve.com.

Brigada: http://www.xc.org/brigada/ Missions & General Christian interest e-mail conferences. Send an e-mail message to Internet: hub@xc.org with the following message:
> *subscribe brigada.*
> *conferences.*
> *help.*
> *end.*

Caleb Project: http://www.goshen.net/calebproject/ — Information on unreached people groups and mobilisation helps.

Global Glimpse: A free weekly e-mail news paragraph. Request a subscription from jhanna@cproject.com.

Global Prayer Digest by E-mail: Receive the GPD free each day by e-mail. Send the following message to Internet: hub@xc.org: subscribe brigada-pubs-globalprayerdigest.

MissionNet: www.associate.com/MissionNet/ E-mail conference for missions related topics. Send subscription requests to Internet: MissionNet@Associate.com.

Agencies and Organisations

AD2000 and Beyond Movement, 2860 S. Circle Dr., Suite 2112, Colorado Springs, CO 80906, Phone: 1-719-576-2000, Fax: 1-719-576-2685, Internet: lauri@ad2000.org.

Adopt-A-People Clearinghouse, PO Box 17490; Colorado Springs, CO 80935-7490; Phone: 1-719-574-7001, Fax: 1-719-574-7005.

AIMS Deutschland, Kerstin Hack, Postfach 45 01 29, 12171 Berlin, Germany, Phone: 49-30-7689-0445, Fax: 49-30-7689-0448, E-mail: 100711.2622@Compuserve.com.

Assemblies of God World Missions (Australia), Chris Aiton, PO Box 254, Mitcham, Victoria 3132, Australia, Phone: 61-3-9872-4566, Fax: 61-3-9872 3220, Internet: cjawm@werple.mira.net.au, http://www.teksupport.net.au/~aogwm/.

Buro fur Weltmission, Jugend mit einer Mission, Mr. Jan Schlegel, 29646 Bispingen, Germany, Phone: 49-5194-1381, Fax: 49-5194-7033, E-mail: 100330.2724@Compuserve.com.

Caleb Project, 10 West Dry Creek Circle, Littleton, CO 80120, USA. Phone: 1-303-730-4170, Fax: 1-303-730-4177, Internet: info@cproject.com.

Centre for Missions Direction, PO Box 31-146, Christchurch 8030, New Zealand, Bob Hall, Phone: 64-3-342-7711, Internet: BobHall@xc.org.

Christian Information Network, Beverly Pegues, 11025 Hwy. 83, Colorado Springs, CO 80921-3623, USA. Phone: 1-719-522-1040, Fax: 1-719-548-9000, Internet: 73422.3471@Compuserve.com.

Church Growth Assn. of India, S.Vasantharaj Albert, P.O. Box: 512, 13/2, Aravamuthan Garden Street, Egmore, Madras - 600 008, South India.

DAWN (Discipling a Whole Nation) Ministries, 7899 Lexington Dr., Suite 200B, Colorado Springs, CO 80920, USA. Phone: 1-719-548-7460, Fax: 1-719-548-7475. Internet: 73143.1211@Compuserve.com.

DAWN Europe, (handling Europe, Middle East, and parts of Asia), 4-6 School Road, Tilehurst, Reading RG31 5AL, England. Phone: 44-118-9415-558 or 44-118-415-559, Fax 44-118-9412-953, Internet: 100337.2106@Compuserve.com.

DAWN Latin America, Berna Salcedo, 7899 Lexington Dr., Suite 200B, Colorado Springs, CO 80920, USA. Phone: 1-719-548-7460, Fax: 1-719-548-7475.

Global Harvest Ministries, PO Box 63060, Colorado Springs, CO 80962-3060, USA. Phone: 1-719-262-9929, Fax: 1-719-262-9920, Internet: 74114.570@Compuserve.com.

Global Mapping International, 7899 Lexington Dr., Suite 200A, Colorado Springs, CO 80920, USA. Phone: 1-719-531-3594, Fax: 1-719-548-7459, Internet: info@gmi.org.

India Church Growth Research Centre, Post Bag 512 13/2 Aravamuthan Garden St, Egmore Madras, TNA INDIA, 600008. Phone: 91-44-825-5372, Fax: 91-44-825-5372.

India Missions Association, Post Box 2529, 48 First Main Road, East Shenoy Nagar, Madras 600 030 India. Phone: 91-44-617596, Fax: 91-44-611859.

Kursgarden Solasen, Stefan Blomberg, P.O. Box 52, 61821 Kolmarden, Schweden. E-mail: sgt@algonet.se.

National Fellowship, Rev. Susanta Patra, Post Box 11247, 11-D Rammohan Behra Lane, Calcutta 700 046, West Bengal. Phone: 91-33-2447913, Fax: 91-33-2447913.

Singapore Centre for Evangelism & Missions (SCEM), André De Winne, Raffles City, PO Box 1052, Singapore 9117. Fax: 65-291-8919.

Target 2000 (Australia), Peter Brownhill, Internet: 100252.376@Compuserve.com.

Target 2000 Frontier Missions Ministries, Highfield Oval, Harpenden, England AL5 4BX. Phone: 44-1582-463-278, Fax: 44-1582-765-489, E-mail: T-2000@oval.com.

Trinity Christian Centre, Ed & Lai-Kheng Pousson, 27 Woking Rd #02-04, Singapore 0513. Fax: 65-472-1163.

U.S. Center for World Mission & Adopt-A-People Campaign, 1605 Elizabeth St, Pasadena, CA 91104, USA. Phone: 1-818-398-2200, Fax: 1-818-398-2263, Internet: aap.campaign@wciumac.wciu.edu.

YWAM Strategic Frontiers. PO Box 25490, Colorado Springs, CO 80936, USA. Phone: 1-719-495-8748, Fax: 1-719-528-1703.

Why Stop Now?

Here's a Way to Keep Praying for the Unreached People Groups Every Day.

ADOPT-A-PEOPLE

G·L·O·B·A·L
Prayer Digest

September, 1996   Vol. 15, No. 8

Steve Halley

From Seoul to Tierra Del Fuego and from Sydney to Seattle, 50,000 saints are praying for the lost *every day*. Why not join them? The *Global Prayer Digest* is a daily prayer guide for unreached people groups. It is printed in three languages: English, Korean, and Spanish. Imagine what the Lord does when 50,000 people pray together on a given day for unreached Muslims, Buddhists, Hindus, or animists!

The structure is very similar to this prayer guide, so it can be used in a variety of ways. For example, in Papua New Guinea, they copy the pages of the *Global Prayer Digest* and give a copy to several congregations that use them in prayer meetings! You can use the *Global Prayer Digest* for a minute of your private devotional time, or devote an entire two-hour prayer meeting to a given issue. Contact one of the following offices for subscription information.

Korean: Kwon Jee Hyun, Kings Children, Mapo PO Box 26, Seoul, KOREA.

Spanish or English: Order Processing, 1605 Elizabeth St., Pasadena, CA 91104, USA.

English from Philippine Distribution Centre: Tony Tubiera, Philippine Partners for World Mission, Inc., ACPO Box 128, Cubao 1109, Quezon City, Philippines.

Recieve the Global Prayer Digest for free by e-mail: send the following message to HUB@XC.org:

subscribe brigada-pubs-globalprayerdigest.